LOVE POETRY OUT LOUD

Also by Robert Alden Rubin

Poetry Out Loud
On the Beaten Path: An Appalachian Pilgrimage

LOVE POETRY OUT LOUD

Edited by Robert Alden Rubin

Algonquin Books of Chapel Hill   2007

Published by
ALGONQUIN BOOKS OF CHAPEL HILL
Post Office Box 2225
Chapel Hill, North Carolina 27515-2225

a division of
WORKMAN PUBLISHING
225 Varick Street
New York, New York 10014

Library of Congress Cataloging-in-Publication Data
Love poetry out loud / edited by Robert Alden Rubin.—1st ed.
p. cm.
ISBN-13: 978-1-56512-459-2; ISBN-10: 1-56512-459-6
1. Love poetry, English.   2. Love poetry, American.   I. Rubin, Robert Alden, 1958–
PR1184.L58 2006
821.008'03543—dc22   2006040076

10 9 8 7 6 5 4 3 2 1
First Edition

For Eva Maryette, who read to me

THANKS TO

Elisabeth Scharlatt for remembering, and to Kathy Pories, Ina Stern, Bob Jones, Elizabeth Maples, and the crew at Algonquin. Additional thanks to Liz Darhansoff and the patient librarians at the Jefferson Building and at the Enoch Pratt Free Library. And, of course, to that most patient of librarians, Cathy.

"The world swarms with writers whose wish is not to be studied, but to be read."
—Samuel Johnson

CONTENTS

Why Love Poetry?

I gotta use words when I talk to you," says Apeneck Sweeney, in T. S. Eliot's verse play *Sweeney Agonistes*. And when you get right down to it, that about sums up the reason for love poetry.

Of course, you haven't "gotta use words" in order to love. Anyone who's had a favorite dog or cat can tell you about mute affection, and anyone whose mother served chicken soup when they were sick in bed can testify that it's possible to say "I love you" without speaking. But you can convey only so much with a meaning gaze, a scratch behind the ears, or a bowl of hot soup. Sometimes a kiss or a bouquet of flowers won't do. Sometimes you gotta use words.

It may seem counterintuitive. Love shouldn't require words. The singer-songwriter Elvis Costello has said that "writing about music is like dancing about architecture," an observation that, at first glance, might as well apply to writing about love. After all, love is a *feeling* — it's an intangible sensation, an emotion that each person encounters differently. Written words, mere ink stains on sheets of pulped-up cellulose fiber or pulses of current in a magnetic field, just sit there on the page or screen; how can they be anything more than a poor facsimile of real feelings? What's the point? Why say anything? As Eliza Doolittle complains in *My Fair Lady,* "Don't talk of love, *show* me!"

Still, futile though it might seem, ever since our ancestors in Mesopotamia started marking on clay tablets five thousand years ago, poets have been writing love poems. There must be a reason.

Maybe it's because words have an undeniable power, and writing them down is a way of storing that power to use at the right moment, the way a battery stores electricity. There's something uncanny and scary about being able to translate wisdom from the timeless realm of the written word into the here and now of the spoken word. When Prospero, the master mage in Shakespeare's *The Tempest,* is ready to leave his magical island of exile, to go back to the everyday world and live a human life, what does he do? He commits his book of spells to the ocean's depths. Without the book, he is just like anyone else.

Whoever first said, "Sticks and stones can break my bones, but words can never hurt me," didn't quite get it. On an emotional level, words can hit as hard as any stick; when we name things, it gives us a certain psychological power over them. That myths, legends, and sacred stories are full of prayers and spells and names and magic words testifies that words *do* matter. What you say can become an action just as much as a kiss, a hug, or a slap in the face, even though you're only making noise with air from your lungs and vibrations of your vocal cords. After all, babies don't cry just to hear their heads go off—they do it because they want to make things happen.

The love poems that you will find in this book make things happen too. More than just a poem *about* love, each is an *act* of love. It may seek to seduce or amuse, to plead or flatter, to inflict pain or express pain, or console, but it's not just some elegant abstraction. Most of these poems are written as if spoken from one person to another. Obviously the books I've drawn upon brim with good love poems that don't do what

I'm talking about—poems that tell stories of love gone bad (or good), philosophical musings on the nature of love, self-portraits of the artist in love, and so forth. But for *Love Poetry Out Loud* I have chosen to focus on poems that seek to cross the emptiness that separates two people—the gap that must be bridged for love to be shared.

The poems I've selected were, with a few exceptions, written originally in English. This excludes some wonderful love poems, but translating a poem inevitably changes it, introducing a third person (the translator) between reader and poet; reciting poetry in its original language is probably challenge enough. In this book's predecessor, *Poetry Out Loud,* I argued that poetry is not a *different* language, but *our* language—"only stretched, purged of certain habits, intensified by careful choice, made memorable by pattern and rhythm." That's true of love poetry too, and the selections here have been further intensified by the nature of what they're saying. When I tried out each of these poems, reading them to myself, to my wife, and to friends as I compiled this book, I sought to listen for the voices of the poets who wrote them. I hope you will too.

These are acts of love, launched across space and time, imbued with all the magic and power and artistry that the poet can conjure up. I invite you to read them aloud to yourself. If they speak to you, try reading them to your lover, or to the person you wish to be your lover, or to your ex-lover, or to friends who share your loves, or to anyone else they might speak to.

After all, if you gotta use words, you might as well use good ones.   ❧

—Robert Alden Rubin

I | Silly Love Songs

"Anyone can be passionate, but it takes real lovers to be silly."

— Rose Franken

LITANY

Billy Collins

You are the bread and the knife,
The crystal goblet and the wine . . .
—Jacques Crickillon

You are the bread and the knife,
the crystal goblet and the wine.
You are the dew on the morning grass
and the burning wheel of the sun.
You are the white apron of the baker
and the marsh birds suddenly in flight.

However, you are not the wind in the orchard,
the plums on the counter,
or the house of cards.
And you are certainly not the pine-scented air.
There is just no way you are the pine-scented air.

It is possible that you are the fish under the bridge,
maybe even the pigeon on the general's head,
but you are not even close
to being the field of cornflowers at dusk.

And a quick look in the mirror will show
that you are neither the boots in the corner
nor the boat asleep in its boathouse.

It might interest you to know,
speaking of the plentiful imagery of the world,
that I am the sound of rain on the roof.

I also happen to be the shooting star,
the evening paper blowing down an alley,
and the basket of chestnuts on the kitchen table.

I am also the moon in the trees
and the blind woman's tea cup.
But don't worry, I am not the bread and the knife.
You are still the bread and the knife.
You will always be the bread and the knife,
not to mention the crystal goblet and — somehow —
    the wine.

Variations on a Theme

---

*Renaissance love poetry,
notably the fourteenth-century
Italian love sonnets of
Francesco Petrarca (Petrarch),
often likened qualities of the
beloved to idealized forms
from nature and classical
culture — skin became ivory,
hair became gold wire, and
so forth. Ever since, poets
have been having fun at old
Petrarch's expense. So does the
American poet Billy Collins,
in this fond catalog of his
love's virtues.*

Litany = *A long prayer of
entreaties or a repetitive chant
or list; here, a litany of
metaphors.*

Jacques Crickillon =
*Belgian poet and writer
(b. 1940).*

Plentiful imagery =
*Metaphor often draws a
logical parallel between two
distinctly different things
and provides another way of
seeing them.*

For an Amorous Lady

Theodore Roethke

Most mammals like caresses, in the sense in which we usually take the word, whereas other creatures, even tame snakes, prefer giving to receiving them.

—— From a natural-history book

The pensive gnu, the staid aardvark,
Accept caresses in the dark;
The bear, equipped with paw and snout,
Would rather take than dish it out.
But snakes, both poisonous and garter,
In love are never known to barter;
The worm, though dank, is sensitive:
His noble nature bids him *give.*

But you, my dearest, have a soul
Encompassing fish, flesh, and fowl.
When amorous arts we would pursue,
You can, with pleasure, bill *or* coo.
You are, in truth, one in a million,
At once mammalian and reptilian.

Animal Love

"You're such an animal!" one lover says to another. Ah, but what kind of animal? Theodore Roethke uses the figurative device of simile to offer some possible answers.

Worm = *Archaic synonym for snake.*

SHE'S ALL MY FANCY PAINTED HIM

Lewis Carroll

She's all my fancy painted him
    (I make no idle boast);
If he or you had lost a limb,
    Which would have suffered most?

He said that you had been to her,
    And seen me here before:
But, in another character
    She was the same of yore.

There was not one that spoke to us,
    Of all that thronged the street;
So he sadly got into a 'bus,
    And pattered with his feet.

They told me you had been to her,
    And mentioned me to him;
She gave me a good character,
    But said I could not swim.

Zero Sum

Charles Lutwidge Dodgson's pen name, Lewis Carroll, derives from Latinized versions of his first and middle names, reversed. This poem's full of reversals, too. Dodgson made his living teaching the logic of mathematics, but became famous as the author of one of the English-speaking world's most popular nonsense stories.

In Alice, part of the poem (which reads like a secret message between lovers) becomes a key piece of evidence in the trial of the Knave of Hearts. It's nonsense, though: don't try too hard to puzzle out who "you," "I," "we," and "they" are. With mathematical precision, all its contradictions and oppositions equal . . . zero.

Gave him two = The King of Hearts, judge in the trial, determines that this refers to missing tarts the Knave is alleged to have stolen.

He sent them word I had not gone
    (We know it to be true);
If she should push the matter on,
    What would become of you?

I gave her one, they gave him two,
    You gave us three or more;
They all returned from him to you,
    Though they were mine before.

If I or she should chance to be
    Involved in this affair,
He trusts to you to set them free,
    Exactly as we were.

My notion was that you had been
    (Before she had this fit)
An obstacle that came between
    Him, and ourselves, and it.

Don't let him know she likes them best,
    For this must ever be
A secret, kept from all the rest
    Between yourself and me.

THE LINGAM AND THE YONI

A. D. Hope

The Lingam and the Yoni
Are walking hand in glove,
O are you listening, honey?
I hear my honey-love.

The He and She our movers
What is it they discuss?
Is it the talk of Lovers?
And do they speak of us?

I hear their high palaver—
O tell me what they say!
The talk goes on for ever
So deep in love are they;

So deep in thought, debating
The suburb and the street;
Time-payment calculating
Upon the bedroom suite.

Tantric Tempers

Although they sound like something out of Dr. Seuss, Lingam and Yoni come from ancient Sanskrit and the worship of the Indian deities Shiva and Shakti. Together these male and female forces of nature cancel each other out and add up to everything that exists, a mathematical relationship that Professor Dodgson would recognize, but that might make him blush. Here, A. D. Hope presents them as a formula for domestic disaster.

Lingam = *The phallic (male) essence that symbolizes the god Shiva.*

Yoni = *The vulvar (female) essence that symbolizes the goddess Shakti.*

Arrears = *Debt, with a*
sprinkling of double
entendre.

Layby = *Payment on time,*
but also suggestive.

But ours is long division
By love's arithmetic,
Until they make provision
To buy a box of brick,

A box that makes her prisoner,
That he must slave to win
To do the Lingam honour,
To keep the Yoni in.

The mortgage on tomorrow?
The haemorrhage of rent?
Against the heart they borrow
At five or six per cent.

The heart has bought fulfilment
Which yet their mouths defer
Until the last instalment
Upon the furniture.

No Lingam for her money
Can make up youth's arrears:
His layby on the Yoni
Will not be paid in years.

And they, who keep this tally,
They count what they destroy;
While, in its secret valley
Withers the herb of joy.

Ah, city life! New York, New York! Center of romance, of culture, of sophistication, of fine restaurants, of brilliant people, of dazzling and varied entertainments! Of the occasional cheap date!

Diminution

Notice that everything's small in this poem, including both inanimate (luncheon-ette) and animate (usher-ette) objects. The latter might object to such objectification.

Petite chérie = *Little darling.*

Tangerine = *Originally a Tangerine Orange (from Tangiers) before the name was shortened.*

Le coup de grâce = *The death blow.*

Demitasse = *Small cup.*

Serviette = *Napkin.*

Weazened = *Shriveled.*

To an Usherette

John Updike

Ah, come with me,
Petite chérie,
And we shall rather happy be.
I know a modest luncheonette
Where, for a little, one can get
A choplet, baby lima beans,
And, segmented, two tangerines.

Le coup de grâce,
My petty lass,
Will be a demi-demitasse
Within a serviette conveyed
By weazened waiters, underpaid,
Who mincingly might grant us spoons
While a combo tinkles trivial tunes.

Ah, with me come,
Ma mini-*femme,*
And I shall say I love you some.

Love under the Republicans (or Democrats)

Ogden Nash

Come live with me and be my love
And we will all the pleasures prove
Of a marriage conducted with economy
In the Twentieth Century Anno Donomy.
We'll live in a dear little walk-up flat
With practically room to swing a cat
And a potted cactus to give it hauteur
And a bathtub equipped with dark brown water.
We'll eat, without undue discouragement,
Foods low in cost but high in nouragement
And quaff with pleasure, while chatting wittily,
The peculiar wine of Little Italy.
We'll remind each other it's smart to be thrifty
And buy our clothes for something-fifty.
We'll stand in line on holidays
For seats at unpopular matinees.
For every Sunday we'll have a lark
And take a walk in Central Park.
And one of these days not too remote
I'll probably up and cut your throat.

The Passionate Cheapskate to His Love

Like John Updike (and Sir Walter Raleigh on page 54), Ogden Nash can't resist playing off the opening of a famous love poem by Christopher Marlowe, "The Passionate Shepherd to His Love" (see Poetry Out Loud*), that invites a young lady to enjoy the simple pleasures of rural life. Apparently the pleasures of simplicity ain't all they're cracked up to be.*

Love: Two Vignettes

Robert Penn Warren

LOVE AND ROCKETS

Sometimes fireworks go off, trumpets blare, and choirs sing. Who cares if people look at you oddly? You're in love! Here Robert Penn Warren and Nikki Giovanni exult in the sheer, intoxicating, silly wonder of it all. Can you blame them?

Spume = *Foam.*

Winds = *A verb here (with a long* i*), evoking the image of a watch's mechanical mainspring, with wind wound by the heart.*

1. Mediterranean Beach, Day after Storm

How instant joy, how clang
And whang the sun, how
Whoop the sea, and oh,
Sun, sing, as whiter than
Rage of snow, let sea the spume
Fling.

Let sea the spume, white, fling,
White on blue wild
With wind, let sun
Sing, while the world
Scuds, clouds boom and belly,
Creak like sails, whiter than,
Brighter than,
Spume in sun-song, oho!
The wind is bright.

Wind the heart winds
In constant coil, turning
In the — forever — light.

Give me your hand.

2. Deciduous Spring

Now, now, the world
All gabbles joy like geese, for
An idiot glory the sky
Bangs. Look!
All leaves are new, are
Now, are
Bangles dangling and
Spangling, in a sudden air
Wangling, then
Hanging quiet, bright.

The world comes back, and again
Is gabbling, and yes,
Remarkably worse, for
The world is a whirl of
Green mirrors gone wild with
Deceit, and the world
Whirls green on a string, then
The leaves go quiet, wink
From their own shade, secretly.

Keep still, just a moment, leaves.

There is something I am trying to remember.

Sensations

Warren's poem celebrates the senses — sound, sight, taste, touch, smell — perceptions that all point to something deeper. Read these vignettes like a joyful shout, letting the exuberant sound of the words explode into life. Notice how alliteration (the repetition of sounds at the beginning of words) creates a percussive rhythm.

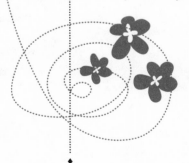

RESIGNATION

Nikki Giovanni

Pop Art

Where Warren turns to exuberant nature for his imagery, Nikki Giovanni draws upon popular culture and contemporary turns of phrase. Here she throws up her hands and "resigns" from the everyday business of acting like a responsible, mature person, giving herself up entirely to the silliness and wonder of being in love.

I love you
>because the Earth turns round the sun
>because the North wind blows north
>>sometimes
>because the Pope is Catholic
>>and most Rabbis Jewish
>because winters flow into springs
>>and the air clears after a storm
>because only my love for you
>>despite the charms of gravity
>>keeps me from falling off this Earth
>>into another dimension

I love you
>because it is the natural order of things

I love you
>like the habit I picked up in college
>>of sleeping through lectures
>>or saying I'm sorry
>>when I get stopped for speeding

because I drink a glass of water
in the morning
and chain-smoke cigarettes
all through the day
because I take my coffee Black
and my milk with chocolate
because you keep my feet warm
though my life a mess
I love you
because I don't want it
any other way

I am helpless
in my love for you
It makes me so happy
to hear you call my name
I am amazed you can resist
locking me in an echo chamber
where your voice reverberates
through the four walls
sending me into spasmatic ecstasy
I love you
because its been so good
for so long

Helpless = *Try reading this poem as if you're someone swept away by the silliness and sensation of pure infatuation. Like Billy Collins (page 1), Giovanni has written a litany of things that might not make sense to someone who's not in love.*

that if I didn't love you

I'd have to be born again

and that is not a theological statement

I am pitiful in my love for you

The Dells tell me Love

is so simple

the thought though of you

sends indescribably delicious multitudinous

thrills throughout and through-in my body

I love you

because no two snowflakes are alike

and it is possible

if you stand tippy-toe

to walk between the raindrops

I love you

because I am afraid of the dark

and can't sleep in the light

because I rub my eyes

when I wake up in the morning

and find you there

because you with all your magic powers were

determined that

"Love Is So Simple" = *Title of a 1968 song by the Dells, a soul group best known for the 1956 hit "Oh, What a Night."*

I should love you
    because there was nothing for you but that
I would love you

I love you
    because you made me
        want to love you
    more than I love my privacy
        my freedom   my commitments
          and responsibilities
I love you 'cause I changed my life
    to love you
    because you saw me one friday
        afternoon and decided that I would
love you
I love you I love you I love you

"O MISTRESS MINE" (*FROM* TWELFTH NIGHT)

William Shakespeare

O mistress mine, where are you roaming?
O, stay and hear, your true-love's coming,
    That can sing both high and low.
Trip no further, pretty sweeting;
Journeys end in lovers meeting,
    Every wise man's son doth know.

What is love? 'Tis not hereafter;
Present mirth hath present laughter;
    What's to come is still unsure.
In delay there lies no plenty,
Then come kiss me sweet and twenty,
    Youth's a stuff will not endure.

NOTHING BUT NO AND I

Michael Drayton

Nothing but no and I, and I and no,
How falls it out so strangely you reply?
I tell ye, fair, I'll not be answered so,
With this affirming no, denying I.
I say, I love, you sleightly answer, I:
I say, you love, you pule me out a no:
I say, I die, you echo me with I:
Save me, I cry, you sigh me out a no;

Must woe and I have nought but no and I?
No I am, if I no more can have;
Answer no more, with silence make reply,
And let me take myself what I do crave,
    Let no and I, with I and you be so:
    Then answer no and I, and I and no.

There's "Yes! Yes!"
in Your Ayes

Drayton's sonnet plays with a Petrarchan tradition in which the beloved is a cruel mistress who torments the lover by refusing him. Here, though, a pun provides the poet with cause for optimism.

Sleightly = *Misleadingly.*

Pule = *Whimper.*

2 | HELLO, I LOVE YOU

"But she was much perplexed by his words and pondered what sort of greeting this might be."

— Luke 1:29

*Love in the abstract is well
and good, but, as songwriters
Nickolas Ashford and Valerie
Simpson remind us, "Ain't
nothing like the real thing,
baby." Perhaps that's why
poets spend their days think-
ing about love and pondering
its mysteries — mysteries that
tend to reveal themselves only
under cover of darkness or in
the clear light of dawn.*

Troth = Good faith.

*Country pleasures =
Wealthy urban families some-
times sent infants off to "wet
nurses" in rural areas.*

Snorted = Snored.

*Seven sleepers = Legendary
early Christian martyrs who
fled to a cave where, like Rip
van Winkle, they fell asleep
and awakened after years had
passed, thinking it only a
night's sleep.*

*Each hath one = The lovers'
worlds are united by possessing
each other.*

THE GOOD MORROW

John Donne

I wonder by my troth, what thou, and I
  Did, till we loved? were we not weaned till then?
But sucked on country pleasures, childishly?
  Or snorted we in the seven sleepers' den?
'Twas so; but this, all pleasures fancies be.
If ever any beauty I did see,
Which I desired, and got, 'twas but a dream of thee.

And now good morrow to our waking souls,
  Which watch not one another out of fear;
For love, all love of other sights controls,
  And makes one little room, an every where.
Let sea-discoverers to new worlds have gone,
Let maps to others, worlds on worlds have shown,
Let us possess one world, each hath one, and is one.

My face in thine eye, thine in mine appears,
 And true plain hearts do in the faces rest,
Where can we find two better hemispheres
 Without sharp north, without declining west?
What ever dies, was not mixed equally;
If our two loves be one, or, thou and I
Love so alike, that none do slacken, none can die.

Awakenings

John Donne (1572 – 1613) lived about the same time as Shakespeare (1564 – 1616). His poems shake up the abstract conventions of Elizabethan love poetry by using striking images from real life (such as a flea or a compass or, as here, waking up in bed with one's lover) to anchor poems about universal themes in particular details.

Good morrow = *Good morning (a salutation).*

Declining west = *During the Dark Ages, the Byzantine, or eastern Roman Empire, was thought to be the center of a world that became more barbaric the farther west you went.*

Mixed equally = *A balance of the "bodily humors" was considered essential to life in classical medicine.*

None can die = *Elizabethans often punned to "die" to mean both death and sexual climax. Here, the arousal will go on forever.*

"WILD NIGHTS —WILD NIGHTS!"

Emily Dickinson

A Dark and Stormy Night

The reclusive Emily Dickinson imagines this night as a storm at sea outside her room, and what it would be like to share her room with a lover. Within the safe Edenic harbor of passionate love, wind and thunder become oddly comforting.

Luxury = *Lust and excess.*

Wild Nights — Wild Nights!
Were I with thee
Wild Nights should be
Our luxury!

Futile — the Winds —
To a Heart in port —
Done with the Compass —
Done with the Chart!

Rowing in Eden —
Ah, the Sea!
Might I but moor — Tonight —
In Thee!

Meeting and Passing

Robert Frost

As I went down the hill along the wall
There was a gate I had leaned at for the view
And had just turned from when I first saw you
As you came up the hill. We met. But all
We did that day was mingle great and small
Footprints in summer dust as if we drew
The figure of our being less than two
But more than one as yet. Your parasol
Pointed the decimal off with one deep thrust.
And all the time we talked you seemed to see
Something down there to smile at in the dust.
(Oh, it was without prejudice to me!)
Afterward I went past what you had passed
Before we met, and you what I had passed.

When you finally meet the one you love, nothing is ever quite the same afterward. The next two poems are about beginnings that open up new worlds through the experience of a kindred soul.

Love at First Sight

In this sonnet, the taciturn Yankee Robert Frost celebrates the wordless connection of two people falling in love. Beneath the polite conversation of two strangers, two souls encounter each other and begin to merge.

Decimal = *The tip of her parasol makes a dotlike indentation in the dust underfoot, becoming like the decimal point in the sum of two people starting to become one. Here, 1 + 1 adds up to about 1.5.*

THE GREETING

R. H. W. Dillard

Bush = *Suggesting the shrub from which God spoke to Moses on Mount Sinai, and of* Euonymus alatus, *or burning bush, a leafy decorative shrub introduced to Virginia that now grows wild.*

Cloud = *Suggesting William Wordsworth's poem, "I Wander'd Lonely as a Cloud."*

Jewel weed = *The seed pods of jewel weed burst open explosively when touched.*

Monarchs = *Butterflies.*

Hello. It is like an echo
Of something I have always known:
From a bush (where you are burning),
From a cloud (you are alone),
The stream's dry whisper, river's slide,
Stone, thistle, the startling leap
Of a jewel weed. I always know the voice.
It is one day hers; one day, his.
Today it is yours.

Hello. And the leaves lapse
Into applause, a flight of monarchs
Dizzies and stills, the high stone arch
Coos with a flutter of doves.
It is like a breeze I have always felt,
Billowing out the silent curtains,
Bumping the pictures on the walls.
One day it is a warm breeze; one day, cold.
Today it is you.

Hello. It is like the face
Of someone I have always known:
The smile of recognition, frown of fear,
Snarl that splits it like a shell,
Blank face of the dreamer, silent dream.
I have always known the dream,
How it lights and flares, how it fades.
It is one day mine; one day, yours.
It is today.

You Had Me at "Hello"

*Where falling in love reminded
the lover of waking up in "The
Good Morrow" (page 22), in
R. H. W. Dillard's poem it is
like entering a dream over and
over. The imagery is that of
the forests and fields of
Virginia's Blue Ridge
Mountains.*

Today = *Which is more real,
the dream or the dreaming?
The poet wonders how we can
hold on to either.*

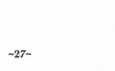

THE LIGHT

Common

SONG OR POEM?

Poets often call their poems "songs," and songwriters often call themselves "poets." Maybe the difference is that a poem must generate its own music, which it does by drawing on traditional forms that readers carry in their heads or on the intrinsic rhythm of the words. A good song, on the other hand, comes across most strongly when helped by melody and instrumental accompaniment, with changes in pitch and phrasing providing another "vocabulary." Consider the work of the next two songwriters.

I never knew a luh, luh-luh, a love like this
Gotta be somethin for me to write this
Queen, I ain't seen you in a minute
Wrote this letter, and finally decide to send it
Signed sealed delivered for us to grow together
Love has no limit, let's spend it slow forever
I know your heart is weathered by what studs did to you
I ain't gon' assault em cause I probably did it too
Because of you, feelings I handle with care
Some niggaz recognize the light but they can't
    handle the glare
You know I ain't the type to walk around
    with matchin shirts
If relationship is effort I will match your work
I wanna be the one to make you happiest,
    it hurts you the most
They say the end is near, it's important that we close . . .
to the most, high
Regardless of what happen on him let's rely

There are times . . . when you'll need someone . . .
I will be by your side . . .
There is a light, that shines,
Special for you, and me . . .

Yo, yo, check it
It's important, we communicate
And tune the fate of this union, to the right pitch
I never call you my bitch or even my boo
There's so much in a name and so much more in you
Few understand the union of woman and man
And sex and a tingle is where they assume that it land
But that's fly by night for you and the sky I write
For in these cold Chi night's moon, you my light
If heaven had a height, you would be that tall
Ghetto to coffee shop, through you I see that all
Let's stick to understandin and we won't fall
For better or worse times, I hope to me you call
So I pray everyday more than anything
Friends will stay as we begin to lay
This foundation for a family — love ain't simple
Why can't it be anything worth having you
    work at annually
Granted we known each other for some time
It don't take a whole day to recognize sunshine

Rhythms of Rap

Rap and hip-hop music sometimes blur the line between song and poem further, because they're often not melodious. Still, the interplay between the rhythmic beats laid down by the deejay at his turntable and cadences of the emcee with his rap is what makes it fun to listen to. This love lyric by the rapper Common (Lonnie Rashied Lynn) will come across aloud most effectively if you read it and imagine a hip-hop beat pulsing away in the background in counterpoint to the rhymes and half-rhymes.

There are times . . . when you'll need someone . . .
I will be by your side, oh darling
There is a light, that shines,
Special for you, and me . . .

Ship hop = *Hop between relationships.*

Yeah . . . yo, yo, check it
It's kinda fresh you listen to more than hip-hop
And I can catch you in the mix from beauty to thrift shop
Plus you ship hop when it's time to, thinkin you fresh
Suggestin beats I should rhyme to
At times when I'm lost I try to find you
You know to give me space when it's time to
My heart's dictionary defines you, it's love and happiness
Truthfully it's hard tryin to practice abstinence
The time we committed love it was real good
Had to be for me to arrive and it still feel good
I know the sex ain't gon' keep you, but as my equal
It's how I must treat you
As my reflection in light I'ma lead you
And whatever's right, I'ma feed you
Digga-da, digga-da, digga-da, digga-digga-da-da
Yo I tell you the rest when I see you, peace

There are times . . . when you'll need someone . . .
I will be by your side . . .
There is a light, that shines,
Special for you, and me . . .

Take my chances . . . before they pass . . .
pass me by, oh darling . . .
You need to look at the other side . . .
You'll agree . . .

"THE TWENTY-NINTH BATHER" *FROM* SONG OF MYSELF

Walt Whitman

Words that Sing

Walt Whitman called these lines part of a very long "song," even though the words didn't rhyme and it wasn't set to music. For Whitman, the term had more to do with an exultant musical attitude than with form — at least not poetic form.

Twenty-eight young men bathe by the shore,
Twenty-eight young men and all so friendly;
Twenty-eight years of womanly life and all so lonesome.

She owns the fine house by the rise of the bank,
She hides handsome and richly drest aft the blinds of
    the window.

Which of the young men does she like the best?
Ah the homeliest of them is beautiful to her.

Where are you off to, lady? for I see you,
You splash in the water there, yet stay stock still in
    your room.

Dancing and laughing along the beach came the
    twenty-ninth bather,
The rest did not see her, but she saw them and loved them.

The beards of the young men glisten'd with wet, it ran
    from their long hair,
Little streams pass'd all over their bodies.

An unseen hand also pass'd over their bodies,
It descended trembling from their temples and ribs.

The young men float on their backs, their white bellies
    bulge to the sun, they do not ask who seizes fast to
    them,
They do not know who puffs and declines with pendant
    and bending arch,
They do not think whom they souse with spray.

Womanly life = *Whitman
imagines a lonely young
woman watching a crowd of
young men skinny-dipping in
a river or lake.*

Unseen hand = *A strong
current of eroticism runs in
these waters, as it does in the
poet, who was homosexual.
Her hand becomes his own in
this song of himself.*

THINE EYES STILL SHINED

Ralph Waldo Emerson

VISIONS OF YOU

Distance and death may keep lovers physically apart, but memories keep them close. Then, in that instant when something sparks a memory and the lovers greet each other again, it's as if time and distance go away, and the vision becomes real.

American Romantic

Emerson is best known as an essayist and philosopher who helped define what it meant to be an American writer. In his poems, he often puts aside that heavy intellectual lifting and focuses on details of nature and moments of perception that connect him to the world.

Evening star = *The planet Venus, associated with the Roman goddess of love.*

Thine eyes still shined for me, though far
  I lonely roved the land or sea:
As I behold yon evening star,
  Which yet beholds not me.

This morn I climbed the misty hill
  And roamed the pastures through;
How danced thy form before my path
  Amidst the deep-eyed dew!

When the redbird spread his sable wing,
  And showed his side of flame;
When the rosebud ripened to the rose,
  In both I read thy name.

SURPRISED BY JOY

William Wordsworth

Surprised by joy—impatient as the wind
   I turned to share the transport—O! with whom
   But Thee, deep buried in the silent tomb,
That spot which no vicissitude can find?
Love, faithful love, recalled thee to my mind—
   But how could I forget thee? Through what power,
   Even for the least division of an hour,
Have I been so beguiled as to be blind
To my most grievous loss?—That thought's return
   Was the worst pang that sorrow ever bore,
Save one, one only, when I stood forlorn,
   Knowing my heart's best treasure was no more;
That neither present time, nor years unborn
   Could to my sight that heavenly face restore.

Double Take

*A poet turns to point some-
thing out to someone he loves,
and all of a sudden it is "now,"
not "then." In this sonnet,
the momentary return of a
lost love shocks William
Wordsworth into recogniz-
ing that, caught up in the
everyday business of living,
he has put aside something he
thought he'd never forget.*

Tomb = *Wordsworth's three-
year-old daughter Catharine
died in 1812. This poem,
which her spirit "suggested" to
him, was published in 1815.*

LOVE'S PHILOSOPHY

Percy Bysshe Shelley

The fountains mingle with the river
   And the rivers with the ocean,
The winds of heaven mix for ever
   With a sweet emotion;
Nothing in the world is single,
   All things by a law divine
In one another's being mingle —
   Why not I with thine?

See the mountains kiss high heaven,
   And the waves clasp one another;
No sister-flower would be forgiven
   If it disdain'd its brother:
And the sunlight clasps the earth,
   And the moon beams kiss the sea —
What are all these kissings worth,
   If thou kiss not me?

POEM

Seamus Heaney

(for Marie)

Love, I shall perfect for you the child
Who diligently potters in my brain
Digging with heavy spade till sods were piled
Or puddling through muck in a deep drain.

Yearly I would sow my yard-long garden.
I'd strip a layer of sods to build the wall
That was to keep out sow and pecking hen.
Yearly, admitting these, the sods would fall.

Or in the sucking clabber I would splash
Delightedly and dam the flowing drain
But always my bastions of clay and mush
Would burst before the rising autumn rain.

Love, you shall perfect for me this child
Whose small imperfect limits would keep breaking:
Within new limits now, arrange the world
And square the circle: four walls and a ring.

Child's Play

"When I was a child," Saint Paul wrote to the Christians of Corinth, "I spake as a child, I understood as a child, I thought as a child: but when I became a man, I put away childish things." For some people, though, putting away childish things is not the mark of adulthood. That seems to be the case for Seamus Heaney, for whom the spirit of that child informs the married man's love.

Sods = *Chunks of peat.*

Clabber = *Of the consistency of curdled milk.*

Square the circle = *An ancient mathematical problem that has come to mean attempting the impossible.*

3 | THE COMEDY OF EROS

"Lord, what fools these mortals be!"

—Shakespeare, *A Midsummer Night's Dream*

PUCKER

Ritah Parrish

DOMESTIC GODDESSES

Love poets have traditionally depicted women as the "weaker vessel"—as the passive recipients or objects of love. Today, reading the old poems, we ask ourselves, What on earth were they thinking? *It was doubtless never true in the first place, and it's certainly not true of the vessels in the next two poems.*

Pomegranate = *A ripe fruit. Compare this, and the beginning of Parrish's poem, to the language of the Song of Songs (page 88).*

My love is deep and penetrating. Subterranean.
Large, thick, slow, deliberate, vulgar, low, archetypal,
   animalistic.
Ripe for splitting open, to be savored, enjoyed.
I am a pomegranate.

And you.
You are everything that ever was
And everything that ever shall be.
I could pray to you.
And, so it begins.

You take me in your arms and fold me like a fan.
You lead me about the room.
My body is pliant, supple.
Your hands stretch wide across my belly, self-assured.

Even your fingers are confident.

We are groveling.
Grinding.
Sinking deeper into it.
Slathering each other with it.

And, then I feel it.

It is traveling through my bowels
Like a vengeful eggplant on fire,
Violently pushing and gurgling its way through my lower
  intestine.
Mocking my sensuality.

For a moment I am shaken.

How can this be? I was so careful at dinner.
Oh God, the cauliflower.
Why? On this day of all days.
The day I wear the crown of woman.

I travel through time.
Suddenly I am 9 years old, in Sister Mercede's 4th grade
  class.
And Christi Ramalo, with her ample bosom and hairy
  upper lip,

Slam Action

This poem by Ritah Parrish comes from the recent phenomenon of "poetry slams," where poets stand up in front of a crowd and duel with words. Slam poems, like this one, often tell stories, play with expectations and conventions, and try to shock by using powerful images or raucous humor. It's not a craft for fainthearted lovers.

Tells me I'm not cool enough to be in the 7-Up club.
And all my mother can say is,
"Honey, sometimes life just isn't fair."

For a moment I fantasize
Just letting it rip.
Will you liken me to some winsome peasant?
Will you love the honesty of it?

Maybe you'll think I'm earthy.

Next, I imagine standing up,
Clutching the bedpost
And proudly declaring,
"It is I, Flatula!"

Would that frighten you, my love?

My muscles tighten
And I begin to pray,
Sweet Baby Jesus
Let your light shine through me and
Neutralize this demon squash-like gas.

I feel an enormous thrust. Is it over?
You cover me with kisses and tenderly pat my thigh.
I tense up and hope for a miracle.
I whisper, "Sweet dreams, my love."
Barely able to contain the steaming monster inside me.

You begin to snore.

I press myself against the wall,
Adhering my buttocks firmly to it
And say twenty-seven
Hail Marys.

I relax for one tiny moment and it moves,
Explodes.
And I am thrown from the bed.
Dear God help me!

A loose chunk of plaster breaks from the ceiling
And flies through the air.
I try to throw myself in front of it.
I try to cheat fate.

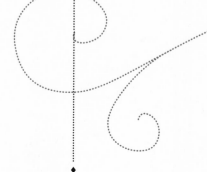

But it is too late.
Too late my love.
The plaster chunk delivers
A cruel but swift death.

I cradle your dented head in my arms and I weep.

I weep for the cruelty of fate,
The loss of true love,
And my lack of muscle control.

I blame myself.

LOVE PORTIONS

Julia Alvarez

We're always fighting about household chores
but with this twist: we fight *to do* the work:
both wanting to fix dinner, mow the lawn,
haul the recycling boxes to the truck,
or wash the dishes when our guests depart.
I don't mean little spats, I mean real fights,
banged doors and harsh words over the soapsuds.
You did it last night! No fair, you shopped!
The feast spoils while we argue portions—
both so afraid of taking advantage.

But love should be unbalanced, a circus clown
carrying a tower of cups and saucers
who slips on a banana peel and lands
with every cup still full of hot coffee—
well, almost every cup. A field of seeds
pushing their green hopes through the frozen earth
to what might be spring or a springlike day
midwinter. Love ignores neat measures,
the waves leave ragged wet marks on the shore,
autumn lights one more fire in the maples.

Unbalanced Love

Here's a portrait of a partnership in which roles are reversed, expectations overturned, and the lovers become dueling jugglers in a carefully choreographed slapstick scene. With, of course, a happy ending.

Tonight, you say you're making our dinner
and won't let me so much as stir the sauce.
I march up to my study in a huff.
The oven buzzer sounds, the smells waft up
of something good I try hard to ignore
while I cook up my paper concoction.
Finally, you call me down to your chef d'oeuvre:
a three-course meal! I hand you mine, this poem.
Briefly, the scales balance between us:
food for the body, nurture for the soul.

Chef d'oeuvre =
Masterpiece.

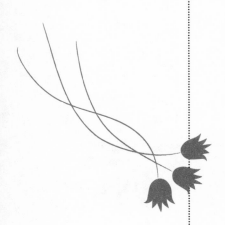

Lonely Hearts

Wendy Cope

Can someone make my simple wish come true?
Male biker seeks female for touring fun.
Do you live in North London? Is it you?

Gay vegetarian whose friends are few,
I'm into music, Shakespeare and the sun.
Can someone make my simple wish come true?

Executive in search of something new —
Perhaps bisexual woman, arty, young.
Do you live in North London? Is it you?

Successful, straight and solvent? I am too —
Attractive Jewish lady with a son.
Can someone make my simple wish come true?

I'm Libran, inexperienced and blue —
Need slim non-smoker, under twenty-one.
Do you live in North London? Is it you?

LOOKING FOR KERMIT

The problem of the one-night stand is nothing new. But in a fast-moving modern culture, finding a prince among all the frogs has gotten much more complicated.

Personal Notice

Unlike the sonnet, the poetic form known as the villanelle is rarely employed for love poetry. It has a long tradition in light and humorous verse, by virtue of its repeating phrases and tight structure. And, though it has been used for serious poems as well, this is not one of them.

Please write (with photo) to Box 152
Who knows where it may lead once we've begun?
Can someone make my simple wish come true?
Do you live in North London? Is it you?

"I, BEING BORN A WOMAN"

Edna St. Vincent Millay

I, being born a woman and distressed
By all the needs and notions of my kind,
Am urged by your propinquity to find
Your person fair, and feel a certain zest
To bear your body's weight upon my breast:
So subtly is the fume of life designed,
To clarify the pulse and cloud the mind,
And leave me once again undone, possessed.
Think not for this, however, the poor treason
Of my stout blood against my staggering brain,
I shall remember you with love, or season
My scorn with pity, — let me make it plain:
I find this frenzy insufficient reason
For conversation when we meet again.

Body Language

The newly liberated post-Victorian attitudes of the Roaring Twenties show up often in the poetry of Edna St. Vincent Millay, who so distinctively employs a formal poetic diction against a context of modernity. In this sonnet the poet's mind is saying one thing, in precise, poetic language; her body, however, says something else.

Propinquity = *Nearness, proximity.*

LOVE SONG: I AND THOU

Alan Dugan

Nothing is plumb, level, or square:
   the studs are bowed, the joists
are shaky by nature, no piece fits
   any other piece without a gap
or pinch, and bent nails
   dance all over the surfacing
like maggots. By Christ
   I am no carpenter. I built
the roof for myself, the walls
   for myself, the floors
for myself, and got
   hung up in it myself. I
danced with a purple thumb
   at this house-warming, drunk
with my prime whiskey: rage.
   Oh, I spat rage's nails
into the frame-up of my work:
   it held. It settled plumb,
level, solid, square and true
   for that great moment. Then

it screamed and went on through,
    skewing as wrong the other way.
God damned it. This is hell,
    but I planned it, I sawed it,
I nailed it, and I
    will live in it until it kills me.
I can nail my left palm
    to the left-hand crosspiece but
I can't do everything myself.
    I need a hand to nail the right,
a help, a love, a you, a wife.

Hell = *For Buber (and,
by extension, for the poet)
love — both divine and
human — is possible only
where subject relates to subject
(I to* thou) *rather that subject
to object (I to* it). *Lovers share
equally in care, commitment,
and responsibility. Aloneness,
estrangement, and lack of
connection become hell.*

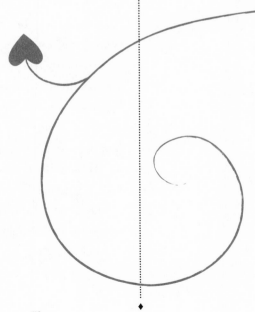

Love Song

Dorothy Parker

Reality Show

*There wasn't such a thing
as television broadcasting in
the 1920s and 1930s, when
Dorothy Parker held court at
New York's Algonquin Round
Table, but here's a love song
that presages early twenty-
first-century cutthroat "reality
shows" such as* Survivor,
The Simple Life, *and* The
Amazing Race, *all rolled
into one. And it's just as real
as any of them.*

Suppose we two were cast away
    On some deserted strand,
Where in the breeze the palm trees sway—
    A sunlit wonderland;
Where never human footstep fell,
    Where tropic love-birds woo,
Like Eve and Adam we could dwell,
    In paradise, for two.
Would you, I wonder, tire of me
    As sunny days went by,
And would you welcome joyously
    A steamer? . . . So would I.

Suppose we sought bucolic ways
    And led the simple life,
Away—as runs the happy phrase—
    From cities' toil and strife.
There you and I could live alone,
    And share our hopes and fears.

A small-town Darby and his Joan,
    We'd face the quiet years.
I wonder, would you ever learn
    My charms could pall on you,
And would you let your fancy turn
    To others? . . . I would, too.

Between us two (suppose once more)
    Had rolled the bounding deep;
You journeyed to a foreign shore,
    And left me here to weep.
I wonder if you'd be the same,
    Though we were far apart,
And if you'd always bear my name
    Engraved upon your heart.
Or would you bask in other smiles,
    And, charmed by novelty,
Forget the one so many miles
    Away? . . . That goes for me.

Darby and his Joan =
*Subjects of a ballad popular
in England in the mid-1700s,
"The Happy Old Couple," by
Henry Woodfall; they became
proverbial examples of peace-
ful and dull married life.*

THE NYMPH'S REPLY TO THE SHEPHERD

Sir Walter Raleigh

CONVENTIONAL
WISDOM

---

*Poems answer and comment
on one another. One of the
most frequently answered is
Christopher Marlowe's "The
Passionate Shepherd to His
Love," which crystallized some
pastoral conventions of clas-
sical and Renaissance poetry.
We've already seen twentieth-
century poets Ogden Nash
(page 11) and John Updike
(page 10) answering Marlowe,
but Marlowe's Elizabethan
contemporaries, including
John Donne and Sir Walter
Raleigh, felt compelled to
answer too.*

Philomel = *The nightingale.*

Gall = *Bile, the "dark
humour."*

If all the world and love were young,
And truth in every shepherd's tongue,
These pretty pleasures might me move,
To live with thee and be thy love.

Time drives the flocks from field to fold,
When rivers rage, and rocks grow cold;
And Philomel becometh dumb;
The rest complain of cares to come.

The flowers do fade, and wanton fields
To wayward winter reckoning yields;
A honey tongue, a heart of gall,
Is fancy's spring, but sorrow's fall.

Thy gowns, thy shoes, thy bed of roses,
Thy cap, thy kirtle, and thy posies,
Soon break, soon wither, soon forgotten;
In folly ripe, in reason rotten.

Thy belt of straw and ivy buds,
Thy coral clasps and amber studs,
All these in me no means can move,
To come to thee and be thy love.

But could youth last, and love still breed,
Had joys no date, nor age no need,
Then these delights my mind might move
To live with thee and be thy love.

Real Shepherds Don't Wear Roses

*The idea of a pastoral Arcadia
where lovers frolic among the
shepherds was a convention
that even the classical authors
admitted was sort of lame; the
Roman poet Virgil introduced
a tomb to the green fields of
his pastoral poems. Raleigh's
"reply" echo's Virgil's theme,
Et in Arcadia ego—
"I [death] too am in Arcadia."
But, if it weren't for that . . .*

Kirtle = *Gown.*

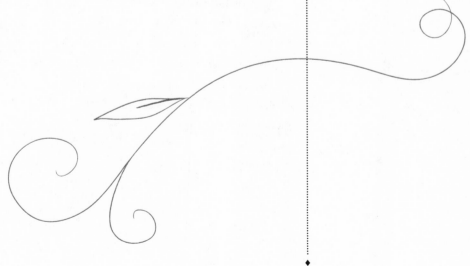

PORTRAIT OF A LADY

William Carlos Williams

Everybody's a Critic

Here's one side of a dialogue between two lovers, or a poet imagining such a dialogue, where the speaker is trying to paint a seductive picture with words, employing the traditions of pastoral hyperbole, and she's having none of it. If you were she, after all, would you want your thigh compared to the trunk of an apple tree?

Your thighs are appletrees
whose blossoms touch the sky.
Which sky? The sky
where Watteau hung a lady's
slipper. Your knees
are a southern breeze — or
a gust of snow. Agh! what
sort of man was Fragonard?
— as if that answered
anything. Ah, yes — below
the knees, since the tune
drops that way, it is
one of those white summer days,
the tall grass of your ankles
flickers upon the shore —
Which shore? —
the sand clings to my lips —
Which shore?

Agh, petals maybe. How
should I know?
Which shore? Which shore?
I said petals from an appletree.

Watteau = *Jean-Antoine
Watteau (1684 – 1721),
French rococo painter of pas-
toral scenes.*

Slipper = *Watteau never
painted a lady's slipper hang-
ing in the sky. The speaker
here has his rococo painters
mixed up.*

Fragonard = *Jean-Honoré
Fragonard (1732 – 1806),
who* did *paint a slipper fly-
ing off a lady's foot, in* The
Swing.

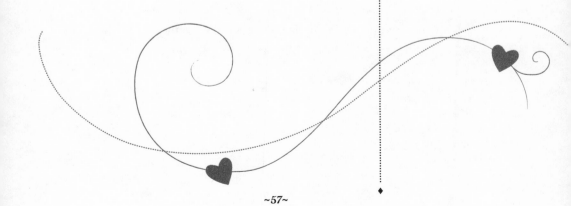

WHERE BE YE GOING, YOU DEVON MAID?

John Keats

NURSERY RHYTHMS

The rhythm of a poem can tell us a lot about its mood. A limerick's rolling meter (known as anapestic) fits its typically bawdy and silly subject matter. The following two poems have a similar bouncy, optimistic, childlike rhythm, like that of nursery rhymes, that touches lightly on love.

Devon Maid = *Keats wrote a friend that "the [Devon] hills are very beautiful, when you get a sight of 'em — the Primroses are out, but then you are in. . . . The Women like your London People in a sort of negative way — because the native men are the poorest creatures in England."*

Junkets = *Dairy desserts set with rennet, a preparation used to curdle milk, derived from the inner lining of the fourth stomach of a calf.*

W here be ye going, you Devon maid?
  And what have ye there in the basket?
Ye tight little fairy, just fresh from the dairy,
  Will ye give me some cream if I ask it?

I love your meads, and I love your flowers,
  And I love your junkets mainly,
But 'hind the door I love kissing more,
  O look not so disdainly.

I love your hills and I love your dales,
  And I love your flocks a-bleating —
But O, on the heather to lie together,
  With both our hearts a-beating!

I'll put your basket all safe in a nook,
  Your shawl I'll hang on a willow,
And we will sigh in the daisy's eye,
  And kiss on a grass-green pillow.

A Roll in the Hay

*It is spring, and you are a
young poet visiting the coast
of Devonshire to take care of a
sick brother, who may be dying
of tuberculosis. So you get out
of doors, and your thoughts
turn to . . . well . . . not to
your sick brother.*

Ye = *Notice how Keats uses
this in the first stanza, when
speaking directly to the girl,
and not in the latter three, as
his imagination takes flight.
In early modern English,
"thee" and "thou" were consid-
ered familiar forms of address,
and "you" was more formal —
the opposite of today's usage.
Th — from the Old English
rune Þ ("thorn") — was often
written as y. In Keats's time,
in more isolated parts of
England, such as Yorkshire
and Devonshire, country folk
still used the old forms of
address. Try reading "ye"
as "thee."*

Daisy's eye = *The sun (the
day's eye's eye).*

BROWN PENNY

W. B. Yeats

Flipping a Coin

*Loves me? Loves me not?
Here's a mature poet looking
back on his youth and a time
when he was falling in love
with a woman he would pur-
sue fruitlessly for years. Was
it all worth it, he wonders? Is
love ever not worth it?*

I whispered, "I am too young,"
And then, "I am old enough";
Wherefore I threw a penny
To find out if I might love.
"Go and love, go and love, young man,
If the lady be young and fair."
Ah, penny, brown penny, brown penny,
I am looped in the loops of her hair.
And the penny sang up in my face,
"There is nobody wise enough
To find out all that is in it,
For he would be thinking of love
That is looped in the loops of her hair,
Till the loops of time had run."
Ah, penny, brown penny, brown penny.
One cannot begin it too soon.

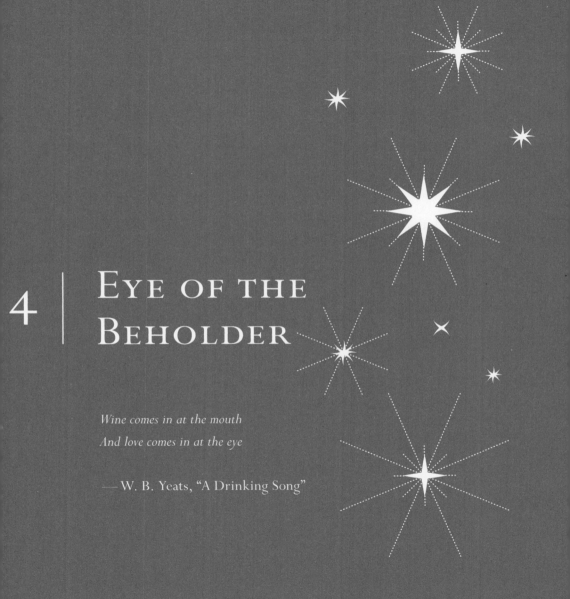

4 | Eye of the Beholder

Wine comes in at the mouth
And love comes in at the eye

— W. B. Yeats, "A Drinking Song"

---

*"I only have eyes for you,"
goes the song, describing
the intense attraction that
sometimes makes otherwise
reasonable people take leave
of their senses. Whether for a
night on the town or a lifetime
together, it's a passion worth
capturing in words.*

Moral Blazon

---

*One traditional form of
love poetry is a "blazon," a
listing of the beloved's
qualities. Browning puts a
twist on the old formula by
showing the moral effect her
beloved has on her — he
makes her a better person.*

Griefs = *Her love affair and
secret marriage to the poet
Robert Browning freed her
from life as a homebound
invalid.*

Lost saints = *The remem-
bered deaths of her mother
and brother.*

How Do I Love Thee?

Elizabeth Barrett Browning

How do I love thee? Let me count the ways.
I love thee to the depth and breadth and height
My soul can reach, when feeling out of sight
For the ends of Being and ideal Grace.
I love thee to the level of everyday's
Most quiet need, by sun and candle-light.
I love thee freely, as men strive for Right;
I love thee purely, as they turn from Praise.
I love thee with the passion put to use
In my old griefs, and with my childhood's faith.
I love thee with a love I seemed to lose
With my lost saints, — I love thee with the breath,
Smiles, tears, of all my life! — and, if God choose,
I shall but love thee better after death.

JUKE BOX LOVE SONG

Langston Hughes

I could take the Harlem night
and wrap around you,
Take the neon lights and make a crown,
Take the Lenox Avenue busses,
Taxis, subways,
And for your love song tone their rumble down.
Take Harlem's heartbeat,
Make a drumbeat,
Put it on a record, let it whirl,
And while we listen to it play,
Dance with you till day—
Dance with you, my sweet brown Harlem girl.

Broadway
Boogie-Woogie

*Langston Hughes often sought
to catch the cadences of blues
music in his poetry, and he
certainly does in this one, a
vignette of Harlem at night in
the mid-twentieth century.*

Tone = *Read it as a verb, to
tone . . . down.*

TO MY DEAR AND LOVING HUSBAND

Anne Bradstreet

STRANGE SHORES

Anne Bradstreet didn't want to go to America in 1630, when her husband decided to do so, because it meant leaving behind civilized English society at age eighteen to raise a family on the frontier in the Massachusetts Bay Colony. She went out of love and a sense of duty. Centuries later John Berryman wonders how.

Love and Money

Marriage is a bargain between two people, and this sonnet by Bradstreet (ca. 1612 – 1672) is framed in terms of value received. She values his love more than money, and that's all she asks of him in order to deal with the trials of colonial life.

Ought but = *Other than.*

Persever = *Persevere; pronounce it "per-sever."*

If ever two were one, then surely we.
If ever man were loved by wife, then thee;
If ever wife was happy in a man,
Compare with me ye women if you can.
I prize thy love more than whole mines of gold,
Or all the riches that the East doth hold.
My love is such that rivers cannot quench,
Nor ought but love from thee, give recompense.
Thy love is such I can no way repay,
The heavens reward thee manifold, I pray.
Then while we live, in love let's so persever,
That when we live no more, we may live ever.

from HOMAGE TO MISTRESS BRADSTREET

John Berryman

1

The Governor your husband lived so long
moved you not, restless, waiting for him? Still,
you were a patient woman—
I seem to see you pause here still:
Sylvester, Quarles, in moments odd you pored
before a fire at, bright eyes on the Lord,
all the children still.
"Simon . . ." Simon will listen while you read a Song.

2

Outside the New World winters in grand dark
white air lashing high thro' the virgin stands
foxes down foxholes sigh,
surely the English heart quails, stunned.
I doubt if Simon than this blast, that sea,
spares from his rigour for your poetry
more. We are on each other's hands
who care. Both of our worlds unhanded us. Lie stark,

Love across the
Centuries

*After reading the poems,
journals, and letters of Anne
Bradstreet, three hundred
years later, John Berryman
writes a love letter to her
ghost. He later said he began
it thinking it would be seven
or eight stanzas long, but
ended up writing fifty-seven
stanzas. Here are the first
three.*

Governor = *Her husband,
Simon Bradstreet (1603 –
1697), governor of the colony
after her death.*

Sylvester, Quarles =
*Favorite writers of
Bradstreet's.*

3

thy eyes look to me mild. Out of maize & air
your body's made, and moves. I summon, see,
from the centuries it.
I think you won't stay. How do we
linger, diminished, in our lovers' air,
implausibly visible, to whom, a year,
years, over interims; or not;
to a long stranger; or not; shimmer and disappear.

Song: To Celia

Ben Jonson

Drink to me only with thine eyes,
    And I will pledge with mine;
Or leave a kiss but in the cup,
    And I'll not look for wine.
The thirst that from the soul doth rise
    Doth ask a drink divine:
But might I of Jove's nectar sup,
    I would not change for thine.
I sent thee, late, a rosy wreath,
    Not so much honouring thee,
As giving it a hope that there
    It could not withered be.
But thou thereon didst only breathe
    And sent'st it back to me,
Since when it grows, and smells, I swear,
    Not of itself, but thee.

ROSY SCENARIOS

When you follow the florist's advice and "say it with roses," you're not only sending flowers, you're sending a message. Roses have traditionally been associated with blood and soul, and both carnal and spiritual love.

Flirting

There's a long poetic tradition in which the poet, constrained by good manners, politics, and jealous rivals or parents, can't come out and say what he means openly. Look for secret messages.

Jove = *Jupiter in Roman mythology.*

Wreath = *A classical symbol of victory and celebration.*

Sent'st it back = *Refused it.*

A Red, Red Rose

Robert Burns

O my luve's like a red, red rose,
　　That's newly sprung in June;
O my luve's like the melodie
　　That's sweetly played in tune.

As fair art thou, my bonnie lass,
　　So deep in luve am I;
And I will luve thee still, my dear,
　　Till a' the seas gang dry.

Till a' the seas gang dry, my dear,
　　And the rocks melt wi' the sun;
And I will luve thee still, my dear,
　　While the sands o' life shall run.

And fare thee weel, my only luve!
　　And fare thee weel a while!
And I will come again, my luve,
　　Tho' it were ten thousand mile!

Ask Me No More

Thomas Carew

Ask me no more where Jove bestows,
When June is past, the fading rose;
For in your beauty's orient deep
These flowers, as in their causes, sleep.

Ask me no more whither do stray
The golden atoms of the day,
For, in pure love, heaven did prepare
Those powders to enrich your hair.

Ask me no more whither doth haste
The nightingale when May is past;
For in your sweet dividing throat
She winters, and keeps warm her note.

Ask me no more where those stars light
That downwards fall in dead of night,
For in your eyes they sit, and there
Fixèd become as in their sphere.

Causes = *The beloved's beauty gives rise to flowers.*

Atoms = *The particles of dust that twinkle in sunbeams.*

Dividing throat = *When the beloved sings or speaks.*

Sphere = *In the Ptolemaic conception of the universe, a sphere of fixed stars lay beyond the sun and planets.*

Phoenix = *The mythical firebird associated with the sun.*

Ask me no more if east or west
The phoenix builds her spicy nest;
For unto you at last she flies,
And in your fragrant bosom dies.

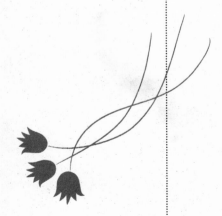

A Girl in a Library

Randall Jarrell

An object among dreams, you sit here with your
   shoes off
And curl your legs up under you; your eyes
Close for a moment, your face moves toward sleep . . .
You are very human.
                But my mind, gone out in tenderness,
Shrinks from its object with a thoughtful sigh.
This is a waist the spirit breaks its arm on.
The gods themselves, against you, struggle in vain.
This broad low strong-boned brow; these heavy eyes;
These calves, grown muscular with certainties;
This nose, three medium-sized pink strawberries
— But I exaggerate. In a little you will leave:
I'll hear, half squeal, half shriek, your laugh of greeting —
Then, *decrescendo*, bars of that strange speech
In which each sound sets out to seek each other,
Murders its own father, marries its own mother,
And ends as one grand transcendental vowel.

The Books of Love

What college student hasn't dozed off while studying in a carrel at the library? A dangerous business, that! You never know when some tweedy English professor is going to spot you snoozing there, fall in love, and make a poem out of you — a poem about waking you up from your dreamy childhood into an enlightened, but somehow more terrible, life as an adult.

Waist = *The girl is no classical beauty, though the poet nevertheless finds her charming.*

Decrescendo, bars = *Musical terms that bring to mind an operatic aria.*

Murders = *Oedipus, subject of an opera by Igor Stravinsky based on the ancient Greek play by Sophocles, murdered his father and married his mother, not knowing who they were.*

Egyptian Helen = An opera by Richard Strauss; one version of the Helen of Troy story held that she never actually reached Troy.

Brünnhilde = Soprano role in Richard Wagner's four-opera cycle The Ring of the Nibelungen.

Salome = Title role of another Strauss opera.

What doest thou here? = God's question of the prophet Elijah, who was hiding in a cave in 1 Kings 19:9.

(Yet for all I know, the Egyptian Helen spoke so.)
As I look, the world contracts around you:
I see Brünnhilde had brown braids and glasses
She used for studying; Salome straight brown bangs,
A calf's brown eyes, and sturdy light-brown limbs
Dusted with cinnamon, an apple-dumpling's . . .
Many a beast has gnawn a leg off and got free,
Many a dolphin curved up from Necessity —
The trap has closed about you, and you sleep.
If someone questioned you, *What doest thou here?*
You'd knit your brows like an orangoutang
(But not so sadly; not so thoughtfully)
And answer with a pure heart, guilelessly:
I'm studying. . . .
               If only you were not!
Assignments,
               recipes,
                              the *Official Rulebook*
Of Basketball — ah, let them go; you needn't mind.
The soul has no assignments, neither cooks
Nor referees: it wastes its time.
                              It wastes its time.
Here in this enclave there are centuries
For you to waste: the short and narrow stream

Of life meanders into a thousand valleys
Of all that was, or might have been, or is to be.
The books, just leafed through, whisper endlessly . . .
Yet it is hard. One sees in your blurred eyes
The "uneasy half-soul" Kipling saw in dogs.
One sees it, in the glass, in one's own eyes.
In rooms alone, in galleries, in libraries,
In tears, in searchings of the heart, in staggering joys
We memorize once more our old creation,
Humanity: with what yawns the unwilling
Flesh puts on its spirit, O my sister!

So many dreams! And not one troubles
Your sleep of life? no self stares shadowily
From these worn hexahedrons, beckoning
With false smiles, tears? . . .
                    Meanwhile Tatyana
Larina (gray eyes nickel with the moonlight
That falls through the willows onto Lensky's tomb;
Now young and shy, now old and cold and sure)
Asks, smiling: "But what is she dreaming of, fat thing?"
I answer: She's not fat. She isn't dreaming.
She purrs or laps or runs, all in her sleep;
Believes, awake, that she is beautiful;
She never dreams.

Half-soul = *A misquotation of Kipling's poem in which a dog prays to his god (his master) and complains about his "distressed half-soul."*

Worn hexahedrons = *Books (their geometrical shape).*

Tatyana Larina = *Jarrell imagines talking about the girl to this character in Alexander Pushkin's novel* Eugene Onegin, *herself a country girl who becomes a sophisticated lady after Lensky, the lover of a friend, dies in a duel.*

Sunset = *In old age, youth's rosy clouds drift away, and we begin to see who we are.*

Lydian mode = *A musical scale resembling a major chord.*

Wooden Mean = *The "golden mean" of classical geometry is considered a perfect proportion; she's not perfect.*

Those sunrise-colored clouds
Around man's head — that inconceivable enchantment
From which, at sunset, we come back to life
To find our graves dug, families dead, selves dying:
Of all this, Tanya, she is innocent.
For nineteen years she's faced reality:
They look alike already.

They say, man wouldn't be
The best thing in this world — and isn't he? —
If he were not too good for it. But she
— She's good enough for it.
And yet sometimes
Her sturdy form, in its pink strapless formal,
Is as if bathed in moonlight — modulated
Into a form of joy, a Lydian mode;
This Wooden Mean's a kind, furred animal
That speaks, in the Wild of things, delighting riddles
To the soul that listens, trusting . . .
Poor senseless Life:
When, in the last light sleep of dawn, the messenger
Comes with his message, you will not awake.
He'll give his feathery whistle, shake you hard,
You'll look with wide eyes at the dewy yard
And dream, with calm slow factuality:

"Today's Commencement. My bachelor's degree
In Home Ec., my doctorate of philosophy
In Phys. Ed.

     [Tanya, they won't even *scan*]
Are waiting for me. . . . "

        Oh, Tatyana,
The Angel comes: better to squawk like a chicken
Than to say with truth, "But I'm a *good* girl,"
And Meet his Challenge with a last firm strange
Uncomprehending smile; and — then, then! — see
The blind date that has stood you up: your life.
(For all this, if it isn't, perhaps, life,
Has yet, at least, a language of its own
Different from the books'; worse than the books'.)
And yet, the ways we miss our lives are life.
Yet . . . yet . . .

     to have one's life add up to *yet!*

You sigh a shuddering sigh. Tatyana murmurs,
"Don't cry, little peasant"; leaves us with a swift
"Good-bye, good-bye . . . Ah, don't think ill of me . . . "
Your eyes open: you sit here thoughtlessly.

Angel = *Jarrell likens gradu-*
ation, and being thrust into
the "real world," to the touch
of the angel of death.

Blind date = *Life's*
disappointments.

I love you — and yet — and yet — I love you.

Don't cry, little peasant. Sit and dream.

One comes, a finger's width beneath your skin,

To the braided maidens singing as they spin;

There sound the shepherd's pipe, the watchman's rattle

Across the short dark distance of the years.

I am a thought of yours: and yet, you do not think . . .

The firelight of a long, blind, dreaming story

Lingers upon your lips; and I have seen

Firm, fixed forever in your closing eyes,

The Corn King beckoning to his Spring Queen.

"Not marble nor the gilded monuments"

William Shakespeare

Not marble nor the gilded monuments
Of princes shall outlive this pow'rful rhyme,
But you shall shine more bright in these contents
Than unswept stone, besmear'd with sluttish time.
When wasteful war shall statues overturn,
And broils root out the work of masonry,
Nor Mars his sword nor war's quick fire shall burn
The living record of your memory.
'Gainst death and all-oblivious enmity
Shall you pace forth; your praise shall still find room,
Even in the eyes of all posterity
That wear this world out to the ending doom.
 So till the judgment that yourself arise,
 You live in this, and dwell in lovers' eyes.

IMMORTAL VERSE

A traditional theme of love poets that shows up often in Shakespeare's sonnets is the immortalizing of the beloved's temporal beauty through the poet's eyes. Archibald MacLeish can't help agreeing, while seeming to argue with Shakespeare and scoff at such sentiments.

Museum of Antiquities

The Venus de Milo, a famous Greek statue of Aphrodite that now shelters in the Louvre, is a byword for classical beauty. But she's missing the arms her sculptor gave her. She had not yet been discovered when Shakespeare wrote this sonnet, but he might say she proves his point.

Sluttish = *Slovenly and grimy.*

Broils = *Disturbances (from freezing and thawing).*

Shakespeare
Was a Liar

Shakespeare's sonnet, if you read carefully, says nothing about what his beloved actually looks like. And so, MacLeish suggests, we have indeed forgotten her. Instead, he shows us concrete images of his beloved — the particular way she walks, the color of her lips, a leaf in her hair, so that we too may catch a glimpse of the "now" he knew when writing this.

Istrian = *Region near Trieste on the Adriatic Sea.*

"Not Marble nor the Gilded Monuments"

Archibald MacLeish

(for Adele)

The praisers of women in their proud and beautiful
poems,
Naming the grave mouth and the hair and the eyes,
Boasted those they loved should be forever remembered:
These were lies.

The words sound but the face in the Istrian sun is
forgotten.
The poet speaks but to her dead ears no more.
The sleek throat is gone — and the breast that was
troubled to listen:
Shadow from door.

Therefore I will not praise your knees nor your fine
walking
Telling you men shall remember your name as long
As lips move or breath is spent or the iron of English
Rings from a tongue.

I shall say you were young, and your arms straight, and
    your mouth scarlet:
I shall say you will die and none will remember you:
Your arms change, and none remember the swish of your
    garments,
Nor the click of your shoe.

Not with my hand's strength, not with difficult labor
Springing the obstinate words to the bones of your breast
And the stubborn line to your young stride and the breath
    to your breathing
And the beat to your haste
Shall I prevail on the hearts of unborn men to remember.

(What is a dead girl but a shadowy ghost
Or a dead man's voice but a distant and vain affirmation
Like dream words most)

Therefore I will not speak of the undying glory of women.
I will say you were young and straight and your skin fair
And you stood in the door and the sun was a shadow of
    leaves on your shoulders
And a leaf on your hair —

I will not speak of the famous beauty of dead women:
I will say the shape of a leaf lay once on your hair.
Till the world ends and the eyes are out and the mouths
  broken
Look! It is there!

5 | LOVES ME

"To fall in love is by no means the most stupid thing man does — gravitation cannot be held responsible, however."

Albert Einstein

*Who doesn't want to be loved?
It's among our most basic
requirements, right up there
with food, water, and safety,
according to the psychologist
Abraham Maslow's famous
"hierarchy of needs." So,
perhaps Christina Georgina
Rossetti and Paul Laurence
Dunbar can be forgiven if they
sound a little giddy.*

Victorian Finery

*Rossetti lived during the
first flowering of Victorian
England's taste for the ornate
and medieval. Much of her
best poetry is about love —
often unrequited love, un-
happy love, and lost love.*

*Halcyon = Glowing and
lustrous, like the feathers of a
kingfisher.*

*Vair = Squirrel fur, often used
in medieval garments.*

A BIRTHDAY

Christina Georgina Rossetti

My heart is like a singing bird
    Whose nest is in a watered shoot;
My heart is like an apple tree
    Whose boughs are bent with thickset fruit;
My heart is like a rainbow shell
    That paddles in a halcyon sea;
My heart is gladder than all these
    Because my love is come to me.

Raise me a dais of silk and down;
    Hang it with vair and purple dyes;
Carve it in doves and pomegranates,
    And peacocks with a hundred eyes;
Work it in gold and silver grapes,
    In leaves and silver fleurs-de-lys;
Because the birthday of my life
    Is come, my love is come to me.

THOU ART MY LUTE

Paul Laurence Dunbar

Thou art my lute, by thee I sing, —
   My being is attuned to thee.
Thou settest all my words a-wing,
   And meltest me to melody.

Thou art my life, by thee I live,
   From thee proceed the joys I know;
Sweetheart, thy hand has power to give
   The meed of love — the cup of woe.

Thou art my love, by thee I lead
   My soul the paths of light along,
From vale to vale, from mead to mead,
   And home it in the hills of song.

My song, my soul, my life, my all,
   Why need I pray or make my plea,
Since my petition cannot fall;
   For I'm already one with thee!

Minstrel Show

Many of Paul Dunbar's most popular poems and stories are dialect pieces, written in the style of the blackface minstrel shows popular in America in the late nineteenth century. That paid the bills: Dunbar was among the first African-American writers to make a living from his work. He had another side, though.

Meed = *Wages.*

Mead = *Meadow.*

ROSE AND GERANIUM

An expensive cultured rose and a ninety-nine-cent Kmart geranium — both beautiful in bloom, but also reflective of changing attitudes toward love. e. e. cummings used a lot of modern devices in his poetry (odd capitalization and punctuation, for instance), but the imagery and cadences and sentiments hark back to nineteenth-century poetry. Connie Voisine's poem, on the other hand, belongs squarely in the twenty-first century.

Myself as = *Pause in between, as if there were punctuation.*

SOMEWHERE I HAVE NEVER TRAVELLED, GLADLY BEYOND

e. e. cummings

Somewhere i have never travelled, gladly beyond
any experience, your eyes have their silence:
in your most frail gesture are things which enclose me,
or which i cannot touch because they are too near

your slightest look easily will unclose me
though i have closed myself as fingers,
you open always petal by petal myself as Spring opens
(touching skilfully, mysteriously) her first rose

or if your wish be to close me, i and
my life will shut very beautifully, suddenly,
as when the heart of this flower imagines
the snow carefully everywhere descending;

nothing which we are to perceive in this world equals
the power of your intense fragility: whose texture
compels me with the colour of its countries,
rendering death and forever with each breathing

(i do not know what it is about you that closes
and opens; only something in me understands
the voice of your eyes is deeper than all roses)
nobody, not even the rain, has such small hands

Small Beauties

*Cummings is suspicious of
big ideas, grand abstractions,
and sweeping pronouncements.
On the page, his lowercase
poems convey smallness. Read
aloud, the precise images and
minute detail of his little loves
unfold with vivid particular-
ity. Here, in a twist on clas-
sical love poems, it is the poet
who is the delicate flower, not
the beloved.*

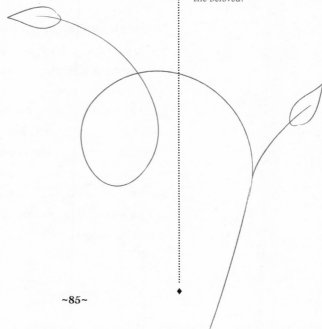

Love Poem

Connie Voisine

Love on the Last Day

A massive airplane roars by close overhead, and for a moment the poet thinks it's the coming of angels at the end of the world—or at least a plane crash. What else comes to mind? A potted plant, hunger, and love.

Angels = Jacob wrestled with an angel (Genesis 32:24–30); in aviation jargon, angels = altitude.

Although the angels of numbers and letters
wrestle darkness into shapes, and the plane
descending over the I-10 wraps

my car in the gust and sonic draw of velocity—
it too has a flight path and calm passengers and no
fiery end for us—I duck and think *so this is it.*

Medievals thought hunger lived its own life in the
body, parasitic, our organs entered by it.
Love was like this too, a contagion, the blood-

filled heart unlocked by his face, her voice,
and we suffered from its side effects of hedonism,
forgetting. The geranium on my porch seems to be

a testament to the finite, the stable, in the warp
of its knobby stems and the slip of white
at each petal's seat, 99 cents at Kmart, but lush

hairs blur the edges of leaves and its musk
supercedes—the water I drink standing near it tastes
heavy and spiced. This flower unlocks, hunger-like,

borders (my mouth, my nose, the water) as does the 747.
Overfull, virulent, the plane dissolves the differences
between my arms, the steering wheel, the airport's

sky and fills me with a roaring which medievals
could only see as dangerous. Animals
killed for slaughter spill their hunger, see how they

continue to bite at the earth? They believed this pour
was absorbed by the grasses and trees, geraniums,
air, and see how much and why I lose myself to you.

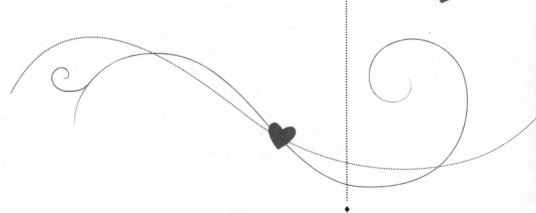

THE SONG OF SONGS (7:1–8:3)

The New English Bible

[Bridegroom:]

How beautiful are your sandalled feet, O prince's
   daughter!
   The curves of your thighs are like jewels,
         the work of a skilled craftsman.
         Your navel is a rounded goblet
         that never shall want for spiced wine.
         Your belly is a heap of wheat
         fenced in by lilies.
   Your two breasts are like two fawns,
         twin fawns of a gazelle.
   Your neck is like a tower of ivory.
   Your eyes are the pools in Heshbon,
         beside the gate of the crowded city.
   Your nose is like towering Lebanon
         that looks towards Damascus.
   You carry your head like Carmel;
         the flowing hair on your head is lustrous black,
         your tresses are braided with ribbons.

How beautiful, how entrancing you are,
    my loved one, daughter of delights!
You are stately as a palm-tree,
    and your breasts are the clusters of dates.
I said, "I will climb up into the palm
    to grasp its fronds."
May I find your breasts like clusters of grapes on the vine,
    the scent of your breath like apricots,
and your whispers like spiced wine
flowing smoothly to welcome my caresses,
gliding down through lips and teeth.

[Bride:]
I am my beloved's, his longing is all for me.
Come, my beloved, let us go out into the fields
    to lie among the henna-bushes;
    let us go early to the vineyards
and see if the vine has budded or its blossoms opened,
    if the pomegranates are in flower.
There will I give you my love,
when the mandrakes give their perfume,
and all rare fruits are ready at our door,
fruits new and old
which I have in store for you, my love.

Love Divine

Many scholars think the Old Testament Song of Songs a collection of ancient Semitic wedding poems, gathered together and attributed to Solomon as expressions of divine love for the chosen people. They seem to be spoken by both a bride and a bridegroom and get pretty racy — probably one reason they're not in the lectionary of Bible readings you're likely to hear in church.

If only you were my own true brother
that sucked my mother's breasts!
Then, if I found you outside, I would kiss you,
and no man would despise me.
I would lead you to the room of the mother who bore me,
bring you to her house for you to embrace me;
I would give you mulled wine to drink
and the fresh juice of pomegranates,
your left arm under my head and your right arm round me.

"If I profane with my unworthiest hand" (*from* Romeo and Juliet)

William Shakespeare

Romeo: If I profane with my unworthiest hand
           This holy shrine, the gentle sin is this,
           My lips, two blushing pilgrims, ready stand
           To smooth that rough touch with a tender kiss.

Juliet: Good pilgrim, you do wrong your hand too much,
           Which mannerly devotion shows in this:
           For saints have hands that pilgrims' hands do
              touch,
           And palm to palm is holy palmers' kiss.

Romeo: Have not saints lips, and holy palmers too?

Juliet: Ay, pilgrim, lips that they must use in pray'r.

Romeo: O, then, dear saint, let lips do what hands do,
           They pray — grant thou, lest faith turn to despair.

Juliet: Saints do not move, though grant for prayers'
           sake.

Romeo: Then move not while my prayer's effect I take.
               [He kisses her.]

A Sonnet for Two

Most Elizabethan sonnets are by a single speaker, professions of a poet's love for the beloved. Here, at the moment when Romeo and Juliet first meet and flirt in Shakespeare's play, their dialogue forms a perfect fourteen-line sonnet.

Pilgrims = Romeo pretends to be a religious pilgrim at a holy shrine.

Saints = The carved images of saints at cathedrals, objects of pilgrimage.

Palmers = In addition to shaking hands, palmers carried palm leaves on pilgrimage. Juliet puns on the two meanings of palm.

Move = Statues don't move when pilgrims touch them.

Now Sleeps the Crimson Petal

Alfred, Lord Tennyson

Whispers in the Darkness

In this invitation to a tryst in the dark, notice the sounds — the breathy open vowels, the sibilant consonants, like a whisper at night.

Porphyry = *Glittering stone.*

Danaë = *In Greek mythology, she was a great beauty, locked up where no man could reach her. But Zeus lusted for her, and came to her in the form of a golden shower. The child of their union was the hero Perseus.*

Now sleeps the crimson petal, now the white;
Nor waves the cypress in the palace walk;
Nor winks the gold fin in the porphyry font:
The fire-fly wakens: waken thou with me.

Now droops the milkwhite peacock like a ghost,
And like a ghost she glimmers on to me.

Now lies the Earth all Danaë to the stars,
And all thy heart lies open unto me.

Now slides the silent meteor on, and leaves
A shining furrow, as thy thoughts in me.

Now folds the lily all her sweetness up,
And slips into the bosom of the lake:
So fold thyself, my dearest, thou, and slip
Into my bosom and be lost in me.

When We Two Parted

George Gordon, Lord Byron

When we two parted
In silence and tears,
Half broken-hearted
To sever for years,
Pale grew thy cheek and cold,
Colder thy kiss;
Truly that hour foretold
Sorrow to this.

The dew of the morning
Sunk chill on my brow—
It felt like the warning
Of what I feel now.
Thy vows are all broken,
And light is thy fame;
I hear thy name spoken,
And share in its shame.

Dangerous to Know

*Lord Byron was characterized
by one of his lovers as "mad,
bad, and dangerous to know."
In his time, he was like one
of today's tabloid superstars,
leaving in his wake a trail
of gossip, broken hearts, and
ruined reputations. Here,
though, it's Byron who claims
to be the injured party.*

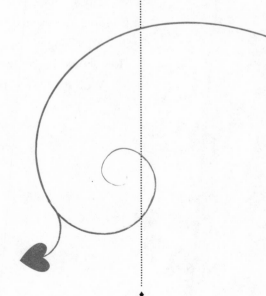

They name thee before me,
    A knell to mine ear;
A shudder comes o'er me—
    Why wert thou so dear?
They know not I knew thee,
    Who knew thee too well:—
Long, long shall I rue thee,
    Too deeply to tell.

In secret we met—
    In silence I grieve,
That thy heart could forget,
    Thy spirit deceive.
If I should meet thee
    After long years,
How should I greet thee?—
    With silence and tears.

"JOY OF MY LIFE, FULL OFT FOR LOVING YOU"

Edmund Spenser

Joy of my life, full oft for loving you
   I bless my lot, that was so lucky placed:
   But then the more your own mishap I rue,
   That are so much by so mean love embased.
For had the equal heavens so much you graced
   In this as in the rest, ye might invent
   Some heavenly wit, whose verse could have enchased
   Your glorious name in golden monument.
But since ye deign'd so goodly to relent
   To me your thrall, in whom is little worth,
   That little that I am shall all be spent
   In setting your immortal praises forth;
Whose lofty argument uplifting me
   Shall lift you up unto an high degree.

YOU MAKE ME A BETTER MAN

Low self-esteem haunts many poets, who are often much misunderstood by the world and their loved ones. Or not. Sometimes it's a pose.

On a Pedestal

Edmund Spenser plays a variation on a common theme of sonneteers, where the poet is ennobled by his beloved's affection.

Embased = *Made plain.*

Equal heavens = *Divine justice.*

Enchased = *To decorate with engraving or gems.*

Thrall = *Slavish servant.*

THE CHANGED MAN

Robert Phillips

Weekend Warrior

We don't think of love poets celebrating suburban domesticity, and indeed Robert Phillips hints that he didn't think so highly of it himself—a self-image problem that new love seems to have cured. Here, then, is the poet as good neighbor.

Pavarotti = *Famed operatic tenor Luciano Pavarotti.*

Scrooge = *From Charles Dickens's novel* A Christmas Carol.

If you were to hear me imitating Pavarotti
in the shower every morning, you would know
how much you have changed my life.

If you were to see me stride across the park,
waving to strangers, then you would know
I am a changed man—like Scrooge

awakened from his bad dreams feeling feather-
light, angel-happy, laughing the father
of a long line of bright laughs—

"It is still not too late to change my life!"
It is changed. Me, who felt short-changed.
Because of you I no longer hate my body.

Because of you I buy new clothes.
Because of you I'm a warrior of joy.
Because of you and me. Drop by

this Saturday morning and discover me
fiercely pulling weeds gladly, dedicated
as a born-again gardener.

Drop by on Sunday — I'll Turtlewax
your sky-blue sports car, no sweat. I'll greet
enemies with a handshake, forgive debtors

with a papal largesse. It's all because
of you. Because of you and me,
I've become one changed man.

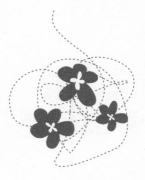

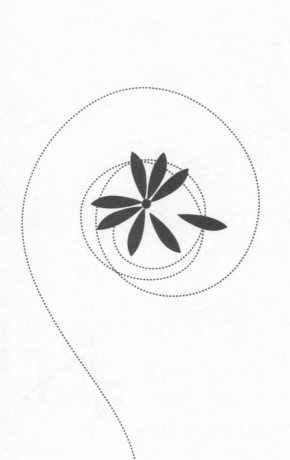

6 | LOVES ME NOT

He was her man,
An' he done her wrong

Mississippi John Hurt, "Frankie"

THEN CAME FLOWERS

Rita Dove

ROSES WITH THORNS

Sometimes there's just no good way to break it off. In these poems, Rita Dove and Aphra Behn let the raw edges show, as they try to maintain their composure in the face of empty gestures by ex-lovers.

Nothing Gold

Chrysanthemum gets its name from the Greek χρυσ-ος (gold), and beneath the showy red-gold flowers its prickly stems make handling it uncomfortable. An appropriate flower, perhaps, for an unpleasant breakup.

I should have known if you gave me flowers
They would be chrysanthemums.
The white spikes singed my fingers.
I cried out; they spilled from the green tissue
And spread at my feet in a pool of soft fire.

If I begged you to stay, what good would it do me?
In the bed, you would lay the flowers between us.
I will pick them up later, arrange them with pincers.
All night from the bureau they'll watch me, their
Plumage as proud, as cocky as firecrackers.

THE DEFIANCE

Aphra Behn

By Heaven 'tis false, I am not vain;
    And rather would the subject be
Of your indifference, or disdain,
    Than wit or raillery.

Take back the trifling praise you give,
    And pass it on some other fool,
Who may the injuring wit believe,
    That turns her into ridicule.

Tell her, she's witty, fair, and gay,
    With all the charms that can subdue:
Perhaps she'll credit what you say;
    But curse me if I do.

If your diversion you design,
    Or my good-nature you have prest:
Or if you do intend it mine,
    You have mistook the jest.

Secret Agent

Aphra Behn was an English spy in the seventeenth century, so she knew deceit when she saw it. Espionage was not very remunerative, though, and to pay her debts she turned to writing plays, poems, and novels, becoming the first woman in England to earn a living with her pen.

Raillery = *Loud joking.*

Diversion = *Amusement.*

Prest = *Imposed upon.*

*Many famous love affairs have
been conducted through the
mail or over the wire, span-
ning oceans and continents.
But in general, distance and
separation do not make for
satisfying relationships. Here
are two poets contemplating
separation, one by distance
and one by time.*

Pass mildly away = *Die.*

Floods . . . tempests =
*Showy conventions of
Petrarchan love poetry.*

Laity = *The uninitiated.*

Moving = *Earthquakes.*

Spheres = *The concentric
spheres that make up the
Ptolemaic universe.*

Sublunary = *Those who live
beneath the moon — ordinary
humans.*

Elemented = *Compounded
from elements.*

A VALEDICTION:
FORBIDDING MOURNING

John Donne

As virtuous men pass mildly away,
　　And whisper to their souls, to go,
Whilst some of their sad friends do say,
　　The breath goes now, and some say, no:

So let us melt, and make no noise,
　　No tear-floods, nor sigh-tempests move,
'Twere profanation of our joys
　　To tell the laity our love.

Moving of th' earth brings harms and fears,
　　Men reckon what it did and meant,
But trepidation of the spheres,
　　Though greater far, is innocent.

Dull sublunary lovers' love
　　(Whose soul is sense) cannot admit
Absence, because it doth remove
　　Those things which elemented it.

But we by a love, so much refined,
    That our selves know not what it is,
Inter-assured of the mind,
    Care less, eyes, lips, and hands to miss.

Our two souls therefore, which are one,
    Though I must go, endure not yet
A breach, but an expansion,
    Like gold to aery thinness beat.

If they be two, they are two so
    As stiff twin compasses are two,
Thy soul the fixed foot, makes no show
    To move, but doth, if th' other do.

And though it in the centre sit,
    Yet when the other far doth roam,
It leans, and hearkens after it,
    And grows erect, as that comes home.

Such wilt thou be to me, who must
    Like th' other foot, obliquely run;
Thy firmness makes my circle just,
    And makes me end, where I begun.

Elements of a Good-bye

A valediction is a good-bye, as any high school valedictorian will probably tell you. How to say good-bye, though, is not something you learn in school. "This isn't good-bye," one lover says. But separation often means the end of love. Donne protests here that such is not the case, that absence only takes the elemental gold of love and makes it thinner, finer, more delicate.

Miss = *It's not a specific part that's missed.*

Compasses = *Two-pronged instruments used to draw circles or measure intervals.*

Just = *A perfect circle.*

When You Are Old

W. B. Yeats

When you are old and grey and full of sleep,
And nodding by the fire, take down this book,
And slowly read, and dream of the soft look
Your eyes had once, and of their shadows deep;

How many loved your moments of glad grace,
And loved your beauty with love false or true,
But one man loved the pilgrim soul in you,
And loved the sorrows of your changing face.

And bending down beside the glowing bars,
Murmur, a little sadly, how Love fled
And paced upon the mountains overhead
And hid his face amid a crowd of stars.

I Will Not Give Thee All My Heart

Grace Hazard Conkling

I will not give thee all my heart
For that I need a place apart
To dream my dreams in, and I know
Few sheltered ways for dreams to go:
But when I shut the door upon
Some secret wonder — still, withdrawn —
Why does thou love me even more,
And hold me closer than before?

When I of love demand the least,
Thou biddest him to fire and feast:
When I am hungry and would eat,
There is no bread, though crusts were sweet.
If I with manna may be fed,
Shall I go all uncomforted?
Nay! Howsoever dear thou art,
I will not give thee all my heart.

A PROPER RESERVE

Society teaches us to hold back something of ourselves, but what's not said between two lovers can become more important than what is. The next two poems are portraits of reserve, one before it becomes a problem, the other one after.

Manna = *Heavenly food that sustained the Israelites in the wilderness when they had no bread.*

Seduced and Abandoned?

As a means of self-preservation, the speaker in Conkling's poem resists the urge to give herself up entirely to her lover, whom she suspects will discard her as soon as he "solves" her mystery.

NEUTRAL TONES

Thomas Hardy

We stood by a pond that winter day,
And the sun was white, as though chidden of God,
And a few leaves lay on the starving sod;
   — They had fallen from an ash, and were gray.

Your eyes on me were as eyes that rove
Over tedious riddles of years ago;
And some words played between us to and fro
   On which lost the more by our love.

The smile on your mouth was the deadest thing
Alive enough to have strength to die;
And a grin of bitterness swept thereby
   Like an ominous bird a-wing. . . .

Since then, keen lessons that love deceives,
And wrings with wrong, have shaped to me
Your face, and the God-curst sun, and a tree,
   And a pond edged with grayish leaves.

"I HEAR AN ARMY CHARGING UPON THE LAND"

James Joyce

I hear an army charging upon the land,
  And the thunder of horses plunging, foam about their
    knees:
Arrogant, in black armor, behind them stand,
  Disdaining the reins, with fluttering whips, the
    charioteers.

They cry unto the night their battle-name:
  I moan in sleep when I hear afar their whirling
    laughter.
They cleave the gloom of dreams, a blinding flame,
  Clanging, clanging upon the heart as upon an anvil.

They come shaking in triumph their long green hair:
  They come out of the sea and run shouting by the
    shore.
My heart, have you no wisdom thus to despair?
  My love, my love, my love, why have you left me
    alone?

SOUND AND SILENCE

Heavy metal rock ballads excepted, loud noises and harsh sounds aren't generally associated with tender sentiments. Here are two poems in which the sound echoes the sense.

Bad Dreams

Dreams are often silent. Not this one. James Joyce gained fame as a novelist, but also published two little-known books of verse that are notable for their delicate evocation of sound and spirit. Listen to the sounds of the words in this poem from Chamber Music *and to how they reflect the sounds of a nightmare.*

SILENTIUM AMORIS

Oscar Wilde

Love That Dare Not Speak Its Name

Oscar Wilde, famed as a glib conversationalist and witty raconteur, writes in this poem about being struck dumb by love. With good reason. He had to keep his homosexuality "in the closet." When he was publicly "outed," he was put on trial under sensational circumstances, convicted, imprisoned, and ruined financially.

Silentium Amoris = *The Silence of Love.*

As often-times the too resplendent sun
Hurries the pallid and reluctant moon
Back to her sombre cave, ere she hath won
A single ballad from the nightingale,
So doth thy Beauty make my lips to fail,
And all my sweetest singing out of tune.

And as at dawn across the level mead
On wings impetuous some wind will come,
And with its too harsh kisses break the reed
Which was its only instrument of song,
So me too stormy passions work my wrong,
And for excess of Love my Love is dumb.

But surely unto Thee mine eyes did show
Why I am silent, and my lute unstrung;
Else it were better we should part, and go,
Thou to some lips of sweeter melody,
And I to nurse the barren memory
Of unkissed kisses, and songs never sung.

VARIATIONS ON THE WORD LOVE

Margaret Atwood

T his is a word we use to plug
holes with. It's the right size for those warm
blanks in speech, for those red heart-
shaped vacancies on the page that look nothing
like real hearts. Add lace
and you can sell
it. We insert it also in the one empty
space on the printed form
that comes with no instructions. There are whole
magazines with not much in them
but the word *love*, you can
rub it all over your body and you
can cook with it too. How do we know
it isn't what goes on at the cool
debaucheries of slugs under damp
pieces of cardboard? As for the weed-
seedlings nosing their tough snouts up
among the lettuces, they shout it.
Love! Love! sing the soldiers, raising
their glittering knives in salute.

FILLING IN THE BLANKS

*We need loving, which is not
to say that we always get what
we need. Searching for love
can lead us into some ambigu-
ous places — places that the
word love hides from public
view . . . places that may in
fact contain nothing. Here
are two poems about love and
emptiness.*

The Big O

*What choice have we except to
try to love? That's the ques-
tion Margaret Atwood seems to
be asking with this poem. The
answers may be unsettling,
but still she keeps trying.*

Then there's the two
of us. This word
is far too short for us, it has only
four letters, too sparse
to fill those deep bare
vacuums between the stars
that press on us with their deafness.
It's not love we don't wish
to fall into, but that fear.
This word is not enough but it will
have to do. It's a single
vowel in this metallic
silence, a mouth that says
O again and again in wonder
and pain, a breath, a finger-
grip on a cliffside. You can
hold on or let go.

Deafness = *There's no sound*
in a vacuum.

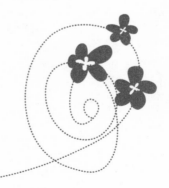

TAKING OFF MY CLOTHES

Carolyn Forché

I take off my shirt, I show you.
I shaved the hair out under my arms.
I roll up my pants, I scraped off the hair
on my legs with a knife, getting white.

My hair is the color of chopped maples.
My eyes dark as beans cooked in the south.
(Coal fields in the moon on torn-up hills)

Skin polished as a Ming bowl
showing its blood cracks, its age, I have hundreds
of names for the snow, for this, all of them quiet.

In the night I come to you and it seems a shame
to waste my deepest shudders on a wall of a man.

Realization

Here's a hard one. You could read it as a poem from a woman speaking to a man, painting a picture of doubt and recrimination after a loveless coupling in which she was never "there" for him. Or you could read it as a woman's words to another woman (one who is denying her feelings for the speaker), a call for sexual self-realization. How would you read it?

Names for the snow = Eskimos are (incorrectly) thought to have many more names for snow than do other cultures.

You recognize strangers,
think you lived through destruction.
You can't explain this night, my face, your memory.

You want to know what I know?
Your own hands are lying.

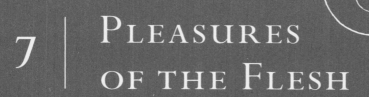

7 | Pleasures
of the Flesh

*"When a man says he had pleasure with a woman
he does not mean conversation."*

Samuel Johnson

WRESTLING

Louisa S. Bevington

ON THE MAT
AND IN THE SEA

The metaphors we use to describe love's entanglements are as many and varied as . . . well . . . the fishes of the sea. So, if you have to ask why a poet might compare lovers to wrestlers or divers, you're probably too young to be reading this.

Victorian-Era Grappling

The American poet Louisa S. Bevington published her work in the 1880s, a century before the steroid-swollen monsters of pro wrestling showed up on our television sets. So, try to picture the lithe athletes of ancient Greek sculpture and pottery; you'll enjoy the poem more.

Twain! = Two apart!

Our oneness is the wrestlers', fierce and close,
  Thrusting and thrust;
One life in dual effort for one prize, —
  We fight, and must;
For soul with soul does battle evermore
  Till love be trust.

Our distance is love's severance; sense divides,
  Each is but each;
Never the very hidden spirit of thee
  My life doth reach;
Twain! since we love athwart the gulf that needs
  Kisses and speech.

Ah! wrestle closelier! we draw nearer so
  Than any bliss
Can bring twain souls who would be whole and one,
  Too near to kiss:
To be one thought, one voice before we die, —
  Wrestle for this.

WET

Marge Piercy

Desire urges us on deeper
and farther into the coral maze
of the body, dense, tropical
where we cannot tell plant
from animal, mind from body
prey from predator, swaying
magenta, teal, green-golden
anemones weaving wide open.

The stronger lusts flash
corn rows of dagger teeth,
but the little desires slip,
sleek frisky neon flowers
into the corners of the eye.
The mouth tastes their strange
sweet and salty blood
burning the back of the tongue.

In Another Element

*We can lose ourselves in the
act of love, an experience
where sex becomes other-
worldly, transporting, raptur-
ous . . . Perhaps that's what
leads Marge Piercy to this
evocation of reef explorers and
the rapture of the deep.*

Deeper and deeper into
the thick warm translucence
where mind and body melt,
where we see with our tongues
and taste with our fingers;
there the horizon of excess
folds as we approach
into plains of not enough.

Now we are returned to ourselves
flung out on the beach
exhausted, flanks heaving
out of oxygen and time,
grinning like childish daubs
of boats. Now it is sleep
draws us down, surrendered
to its dark glimmer.

DOWN, WANTON, DOWN!

Robert Graves

Down, wanton, down! Have you no shame
That at the whisper of Love's name,
Or Beauty's, presto! up you raise
Your angry head and stand at gaze?

Poor bombard-captain, sworn to reach
The ravelin and effect a breach—
Indifferent what you storm or why,
So be that in the breach you die!

Love may be blind, but Love at least
Knows what is man and what mere beast;
Or Beauty wayward, but requires
More delicacy from her squires.

Tell me, my witless, whose one boast
Could be your staunchness at the post,
When were you made a man of parts
To think fine and profess the arts?

Will many-gifted Beauty come
Bowing to your bald rule of thumb,
Or Love swear loyalty to your crown?
Be gone, have done! Down, wanton, down!

Stand-up Comedy

Graves channels the spirit of Elizabethan-era literary wit and low Shakespearean bawdy here, spinning out a series of puns and double entendres that would make Falstaff roar and Mistress Quickly blush.

Poem for Sigmund

Lorna Crozier

Sometimes Not Just a Cigar

Among Sigmund Freud's most controversial psychological theories was his suggestion that female children grow up with a sense of having been castrated and, consequently, envy the male organ and want to possess it. Lorna Crozier finds the whole idea amusing.

It's a funny thing,
a Brontosaurus with a long neck
and pea-sized brain, only room
for one thought and that's
not extinction. It's lucky
its mouth is vertical
and not the other way
or we'd see it
smiling like a Cheshire cat.
(Hard to get in the mood
with that grin in your mind.)
No wonder I feel fond of it,
its simple trust of me
as my hands slide down your belly,
the way it jumps up
like a drawing in a child's pop-up book,
expecting me
to say "Hi!
Surprised to see you,"
expecting tenderness
from these envious woman's hands.

The kiss, the embrace, the act of love——they can be tender, but they are moments of arousal and excitement. Just after those moments have passed, when the rapture retreats and we come back to ourselves and to the loving other who is with us, is when some of our greatest love poetry finds its inspiration.

Slope = *The poet briefly be-comes like the goddess of love, and the view is from the* mons veneris *(mountain of Venus).*

Venus = *In the myth of Venus and Adonis, the goddess be-comes infatuated with a beau-tiful youth, an infatuation that Auden shares.*

LULLABY

W. H. Auden

Lay your sleeping head, my love,
Human on my faithless arm;
Time and fevers burn away
Individual beauty from
Thoughtful children, and the grave
Proves the child ephemeral:
But in my arms till break of day
Let the living creature lie,
Mortal, guilty, but to me
The entirely beautiful.

Soul and body have no bounds:
To lovers as they lie upon
Her tolerant enchanted slope
In their ordinary swoon,
Grave the vision Venus sends
Of supernatural sympathy,
Universal love and hope;
While an abstract insight wakes
Among the glaciers and the rocks
The hermit's carnal ecstasy.

Certainty, fidelity
On the stroke of midnight pass
Like vibrations of a bell
And fashionable madmen raise
Their pedantic boring cry:
Every farthing of the cost,
All the dreaded cards foretell,
Shall be paid, but from this night
Not a whisper, not a thought
Not a kiss nor look be lost.

Beauty, midnight, vision dies:
Let the winds of dawn that blow
Softly round your dreaming head
Such a day of welcome show
Eye and knocking heart may bless,
Find our mortal world enough;
Noons of dryness find you fed
By the involuntary powers,
Nights of insult let you pass
Watched by every human love.

A View from the Mountain

In this moment of vision, the poet finds connection with the particular (the lover in his arms) and the universal (all of creation). W. H. Auden also hears echoes of classical mythology in this intense intimacy.

GREEN

Paul Verlaine

Love in the Morning

What would a book of love poetry be without something in the "language of love"? Since French has a perfectly good word for the color green, and Verlaine didn't call the poem "Vert," the green is probably of the English sort — an open grassy area, planted with flowering fruit trees and shrubs. Your editor's translation appears in brackets.

Feuilles = *Leaves or bracts.*

Rosée = *Dew.*

Front = *Forehead.*

Voici des fruits, des fleurs, des feuilles et des branches
Et puis voici mon coeur qui ne bat que pour vous.
Ne le déchirez pas avec vos deux mains blanches
Et qu'à vos yeux si beaux l'humble présent soit doux.

[About us here are fruit and flower, bract and bough,
And here too is my heart, which beats only for you.
Nor let those pale white hands tear that to pieces now
Which makes so poor a gift for your fair eyes to view.]

J'arrive tout couvert encore de rosée
Que le vent du matin vient glacer à mon front.
Souffrez que ma fatigue à vos pieds reposée
Rêve des chers instants qui la délasseront.

[All dewy am I come to be complete,
With morning's light airs icy on my brow.
Permit me so to lay this languor at your feet,
Refreshed for those rare moments only dreams allow.]

Sur votre jeune sein laissez rouler ma tête
Toute sonore encor de vos derniers baisers;
Laissez-la s'apaiser de la bonne tempête.
Et que je dorme un peu puisque vous reposez.

Baisers = *Kisses*.

> *[On your sweet breast then might I place my head,*
> *Which swirls from your last kisses, long and deep;*
> *And, since our own ecstatic tempest's quieted,*
> *As you do rest a little, I perhaps may sleep.]*

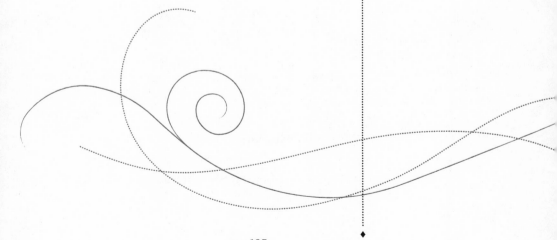

CORAL

Derek Walcott

TOUCH

These two poems are about touch — one of absence, one of presence. For the Caribbean poet Derek Walcott, the imagery is of sea and sun. For the American poet Jean Toomer, the imagery is of a city night, early in the last century.

Salty Like the Sea

In the islands and along the coast, one can find souvenir shops selling shells and coral. The pieces of coral we find in such shops are skeletons left behind by once living creatures. Only in their absence can we grasp them. The poet stops in to look and finds himself transported by touch, reminded of love by its absence.

This coral's shape echoes the hand
It hollowed. Its

Immediate absence is heavy. As pumice,
As your breast in my cupped palm.

Sea-cold, its nipple rasps like sand,
Its pores, like yours, shone with salt sweat.

Bodies in absence displace their weight,
And your smooth body, like none other,

Creates an exact absence like this stone
Set on a table with a whitening rack

Of souvenirs. It dares my hand
To claim what lovers' hands have never known:

The nature of the body of another.

HER LIPS ARE COPPER WIRE

Jean Toomer

W hisper of yellow globes
gleaming on lamp-posts that sway
like bootleg licker drinkers in the fog

and let your breath be moist against me
like bright beads on yellow globes

telephone the power-house
that the main wires are insulate

(her words play softly up and down
dewy corridors of billboards)

then with your tongue remove the tape
and press your lips to mine
till they are incandescent

City Lights

*Washington, D.C., after
World War I, during
Prohibition, was a city at
a threshold, linking north
and south. Toomer was at a
threshold too. In this poem
he evokes that electric time
and place. Try reading it
as a woman speaking to a
man, with the male narrator
speaking in the title and in
parentheses.*

Insulate = *Covered with
insulation.*

It's said that your brain is your most important sex organ. In its ability to attach meaning and beauty to attraction, to rationalize impulses, to imagine what could be, and to deny what is, the brain makes the whole business possible. Here are two good examples of the brain at work, one by a young poet, and another by an aging one.

In labour = *Waiting in pain.*

Tired with standing = *Sexually excited.*

Harmonious chime = *Perhaps a chiming watch, fashionable at the time.*

Busk = *Corset.*

Still = *Erect.*

Hairy diadem = *Her crown of hair.*

"COME, MADAM, COME, ALL REST MY POWERS DEFY"

John Donne

Come, Madam, come, all rest my powers defy,
Until I labour, I in labour lie.
The foe oft-times having the foe in sight,
Is tired with standing though they never fight.
Off with that girdle, like heaven's zone glistering,
But a far fairer world encompassing.
Unpin that spangled breastplate which you wear,
That th' eyes of busy fools may be stopped there.
Unlace yourself, for that harmonious chime
Tells me from you, that now 'tis your bed time.
Off with that happy busk, which I envy,
That still can be, and still can stand so nigh.
Your gown going off, such beauteous state reveals,
As when from flowery meads th' hill's shadow steals.
Off with that wiry coronet and show
The hairy diadem which on you doth grow;
Now off with those shoes, and then safely tread
In this love's hallowed temple, this soft bed.
In such white robes heaven's angels used to be

Received by men; thou angel bring'st with thee
A heaven like Mahomet's paradise; and though
Ill spirits walk in white, we easily know
By this these angels from an evil sprite,
Those set our hairs, but these our flesh upright.
      Licence my roving hands, and let them go
Before, behind, between, above, below.
O my America, my new found land,
My kingdom, safeliest when with one man manned,
My mine of precious stones, my empery,
How blessed am I in this discovering thee!
To enter in these bonds, is to be free;
Then where my hand is set, my seal shall be.
      Full nakedness, all joys are due to thee.
As souls unbodied, bodies unclothed must be,
To taste whole joys. Gems which you women use
Are like Atlanta's balls, cast in men's views,
That when a fool's eye lighteth on a gem,
His earthly soul may covet theirs, not them.
Like pictures, or like books' gay coverings made
For laymen, are all women thus arrayed;
Themselves are mystic books, which only we
Whom their imputed grace will dignify
Must see revealed. Then since I may know,
As liberally, as to a midwife, show

Undressing

We normally think of elegies as somber poems, but an elegy can be any kind of extended meditative reflection. In this case, it's a playful meditation on erotic love, and a request to get busy. Often titled "To His Mistress Going to Bed," it's young John Donne at his wittiest, most rakish, and most unabashedly punny. Indeed, it was too risqué for his literary executors to include in the edition of his poems published after his death, at which time he was an old and well-respected clergyman.

Mahomet's paradise = *The heaven of sensual delights that awaited men, according to Islamic teaching.*

Manned = *Inhabited.*

Atlanta's balls = In *Greek mythology, the swift-footed Atlanta was beaten in a race, and thus won in marriage, when she was tricked into stopping for some golden apples; here, the roles are reversed.*

Thyself: cast all, yea, this white linen hence,
Here is no penance, much less innocence.
    To teach thee, I am naked first, why then
What needst thou have more covering than a man.

Laymen = *The uninitiated;*
a groan is an appropriate
response to the double
entendre.

Than a man =
Also a groaner.

THE AGED LOVER DISCOURSES IN THE FLAT STYLE

J. V. Cunningham

There are, perhaps, whom passion gives a grace,
Who fuse and part as dancers on the stage,
But that is not for me, not at my age,
Not with my bony shoulders and fat face.
Yet in my clumsiness I found a place
And use for passion: with it I ignore
My gaucheries and yours, and feel no more
The awkwardness of the absurd embrace.

It is a pact men make, and seal in flesh,
To be so busy with their own desires
Their loves may be as busy with their own,
And not in union. Though the two enmesh
Like gears in motion, each with each conspires
To be at once together and alone.

Senior Activities

J. V. Cunningham was a fan of Donne's poetry, and it shows in his techniques of versification and in some of the imagery. But instead of Donne's rhetorical pyrotechnics, Cunningham's modern meditation is gently self-mocking and ironic.

8 | WILL YOU MISS ME WHEN I'M GONE?

KANE. *You always said you wanted to live in a palace.*
SUSAN. *Oh, a person could go crazy in this dump. Nobody
to talk to, nobody to have any fun with.*
KANE. *Susan.*
SUSAN. *Forty-nine thousand acres of nothing but scenery
and statues. I'm lonesome.*

— Herman J. Mankiewicz and Orson Welles,
Citizen Kane

The River-Merchant's Wife: A Letter

Ezra Pound

LOVE LETTERS

Instant messaging, Internet chat, voice mail, real-time video, mobile phones . . . who has time to write a letter anymore? More's the pity — love letters have an ancient pedigree, and even now nothing quite says "I miss you" as well. Two lonely voices can be heard in this letter and the one that follows.

While my hair was still cut straight across my
   forehead
I played about the front gate, pulling flowers.
You came by on bamboo stilts, playing horse,
You walked about my seat, playing with blue plums.
And we went on living in the village of Chōkan:
Two small people, without dislike or suspicion.

At fourteen I married My Lord you.
I never laughed, being bashful.
Lowering my head, I looked at the wall.
Called to, a thousand times, I never looked back.

At fifteen I stopped scowling,
I desired my dust to be mingled with yours
Forever and forever and forever.
Why should I climb the look out?

At sixteen you departed,

You went into far Ku-tō-en, by the river of swirling
   eddies,

And you have been gone five months.

The monkeys make sorrowful noise overhead.

You dragged your feet when you went out.

By the gate now, the moss is grown, the different mosses,

Too deep to clear them away!

The leaves fall early this autumn, in wind.

The paired butterflies are already yellow with August

Over the grass in the West garden;

They hurt me. I grow older.

If you are coming down through the narrows of the river
   Kiang,

Please let me know beforehand,

And I will come out to meet you
     As far as Chō-fū-Sa.

Out of Character

*Ezra Pound could not read
Chinese, nor could the scholar
whose research turned up the
ideograms of the eighth-
century poet Li Po, and whose
work with native-speaking
translators Pound inherited.
In finding a modern voice for
a lonely girl from a thousand
years earlier, Pound makes the
poem his own.*

Little Boy Lost

Some men never really grow up (and, arguably, a lot of those who become poets fit into that category). Some women find that quality endearing. Others . . . well . . . Stephen Dunn hopes that the woman he's writing to belongs with the first group.

LETTER HOME

Stephen Dunn

(For L.)

Last night during a thunderstorm,
awakened and half-awake,
I wanted to climb into bed
on my mother's side, be told
everything's all right—
the mother-lie which gives us power
to make it true.
Then I realized she was dead,
that you're the one I sleep with
and rely on, and I wanted you.
The thunder brought what thunder brings.
I lay there, trembling,
thinking what perfect sense we make
of each other when we're afraid
or half-asleep or alone.

Later the sky was all stars,
the obvious ones and those
you need to look at a little sideways
until they offer themselves.
I wanted to see them all—
wanted too much, you'd say—
like this desire to float
between the egg and the grave,
unaccountable, neither lost nor found,
then wanting the comfortable
orthodoxies of home.

I grew up thinking home was a place
you left with a bat
in your hands; you came back dirty
or something was wrong.
Only bad girls were allowed
to roam as often or as far.
Shall we admit
that because of our bodies
your story can never be mine,
mine never yours?
That where and when they intersect
is the greatest intimacy we'll ever have?

Sideways = *The eye's struc-
ture is such that it sees color
best when looking straight
ahead; the "corners" of the eye
see black and white best, and
so can perceive faint stars that
aren't visible when stared at
directly.*

Every minute or so a mockingbird
delivers its repertoire.
Here's my blood
in the gray remains of a mosquito.
I know I'm just another slug
in the yard, but that's not what
my body knows.
The boy must die is the lesson
hardest learned.
I'll be home soon. Will you understand
if not forgive
that I expect to be loved
beyond deserving, as always?

THE VOICE

Thomas Hardy

Woman much missed, how you call to me,
    call to me,
Saying that now you are not as you were
When you had changed from the one who was all to me,
But as at first, when our day was fair.

Can it be you that I hear? Let me view you, then,
Standing as when I drew near to the town
Where you would wait for me: yes, as I knew you then,
Even to the original air-blue gown!

Or is it only the breeze, in its listlessness
Travelling across the wet mead to me here,
You being ever dissolved to wan wistlessness,
Heard no more again far or near?

    Thus I; faltering forward,
    Leaves around me falling,
Wind oozing thin through the thorn from norward,
    And the woman calling.

LETTING GO

"If you love someone," the truism tells us, "set them free." Easy said. Sometimes there's a part of us that just won't let go, no matter how sensibly we argue with ourselves. The next two poets are having a hard time of it.

A Haunting

The life had gone out of Thomas Hardy's marriage long before his wife died. So why, after her death, does he find himself haunted by her? As you read this poem, listen for the way that the ghostly voice echoes and the effect it has on the poet in the last stanza, which falters like the poet.

Wistlessness = *Wistfulness, a poetic word suggestive of both silence and wishing.*

Norward = *North.*

I WILL NOT LET THEE GO

Robert Bridges

Holding On

Weddings traditionally take place in front of many witnesses—for a reason. With all those people looking on, it's hard to take back promises. Here, Robert Bridges argues that the affair that's ending has been in full view of witnesses such as the sun, the moon, the stars, and the flowers.

Scare = Frighten away, undo.

I will not let thee go.
Ends all our month-long love in this?
Can it be summed up so,
Quit in a single kiss?
I will not let thee go.

I will not let thee go.
If thy words' breath could scare thy deeds,
As the soft south can blow
And toss the feathered seeds,
Then might I let thee go.

I will not let thee go.
Had not the great sun seen, I might;
Or were he reckoned slow
To bring the false to light,
Then might I let thee go.

I will not let thee go.
The stars that crowd the summer skies
    Have watched us so below
    With all their million eyes,
    I dare not let thee go.

I will not let thee go.
Have we not chid the changeful moon,
    Now rising late, and now
    Because she set too soon,
    And shall I let thee go?

I will not let thee go.
Have not the young flowers been content,
    Plucked ere their buds could blow,
    To seal our sacrament?
    I cannot let thee go.

I will not let thee go.
I hold thee by too many bands:
    Thou sayest farewell, and lo!
    I have thee by the hands,
    And will not let thee go.

Chid = *Scolded.*

THE MEETING

Katherine Mansfield

We started speaking—
Looked at each other; then turned away—
The tears kept rising to my eyes
But I could not weep
I wanted to take your hand
But my hand trembled.
You kept counting the days
Before we should meet again
But both of us felt in our heart
That we parted for ever and ever.
The ticking of the little clock filled the quiet room—
Listen I said; it is so loud
Like a horse galloping on a lonely road.
As loud as that—a horse galloping past in the night.
You shut me up in your arms—
But the sound of the clock stifled our hearts' beating.
You said "I cannot go: all that is living of me
Is here for ever and ever."
Then you went.

The world changed. The sound of the clock grew fainter
Dwindled away — became a minute thing —
I whispered in the darkness: "If it stops, I shall die."

Promises

*Sometimes people promise
things they can't deliver and
say things just to be saying
them, even though deep down
they know they're not true.
Here, Katherine Mansfield's
rational self knows that,
but all she can hear are the
promises — and the time tick-
ing by.*

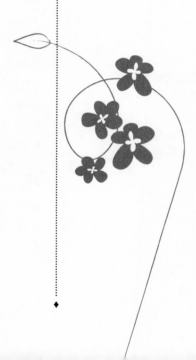

Still Looking Out for Number One

Raymond Carver

Bachelor Pad

Tough guys don't dance, don't care what other people think, and don't get lonely. Oh yeah, they don't write poetry either. Sure they don't.

Now that you've gone away for five days,
I'll smoke all the cigarettes I want,
where I want. Make biscuits and eat them
with jam and fat bacon. Loaf. Indulge
myself. Walk on the beach if I feel
like it. And I feel like it, alone and
thinking about when I was young. The people
then who loved me beyond reason.
And how I loved them above all others.
Except one. I'm saying I'll do everything
I want here while you're away!
But there's one thing I won't do.
I won't sleep in our bed without you.
No. It doesn't please me to do so.
I'll sleep where I damn well feel like it —
where I sleep best when you're away
and I can't hold you the way I do.
On the broken sofa in my study.

BEARDED OAKS

Robert Penn Warren

T he oaks, how subtle and marine,
Bearded, and all the layered light
Above them swims; and thus the scene,
Recessed, awaits the positive night.

So, waiting, we in the grass now lie
Beneath the languorous tread of light:
The grasses, kelp-like, satisfy
The nameless motions of the air.

Upon the floor of light, and time,
Unmurmuring, of polyp made,
We rest; we are, as light withdraws,
Twin atolls on a shelf of shade.

Ages to our construction went,
Dim architecture, hour by hour:
And violence, forgot now, lent
The present stillness all its power.

TIME OUT

Love poems often offer a message that we should enjoy love while we can, since time is passing. But when lovers are apart, time no longer seems to be on their side.

Bearded = *With Spanish moss, an epiphytic bromeliad plant.*

Polyp = *The great limestone structures we call* coral *are actually secreted by tiny animals — coral polyps — that live in them like snails live in their shells. See also Derek Walcott's poem on page 124.*

Black Lagoon

This poem may seem tough to follow, but pay attention: Two lovers watch the sun set and night flow into the landscape. To the poet it seems as if they are coral outcroppings, watching stonily as the tide of time flows into the lagoon and covers them. Imagine it, he suggests to his lover: it is good practice for the way that time will eat away at the solid substance of our lives, covering us ultimately in darkness.

Ruth = *Sorrow and pity.*

The storm of noon above us rolled,
Of light the fury, furious gold,
The long drag troubling us, the depth:
Dark is unrocking, unrippling, still.

Passion and slaughter, ruth, decay
Descend, minutely whispering down,
Silted down swaying streams, to lay
Foundation for our voicelessness.

All our debate is voiceless here,
As all our rage, the rage of stone;
If hope is hopeless, the fearless is fear,
And history is thus undone.

Our feet once wrought the hollow street
With echo when the lamps were dead
At windows, once our headlight glare
Disturbed the doe that, leaping, fled.

I do not love you less that now
The caged heart makes iron stroke,
Or less that all that light once gave
The graduate dark should now revoke.

We live in time so little time
And we learn all so painfully,
That we may spare this hour's term
To practice for eternity.

48 Hours after You Left

DJ Renegade

Einstein Was Right

The theory of relativity posits that time proceeds at different rates depending on where you are and how fast you're going. Anyone who's had to wait for a loved one will confirm it. For DJ Renegade, all sorts of strange things are happening to the fabric of reality.

Mad Dog = *Street name for a potent fortified wine produced by Mogen David.*

The telephone
has put on a bathrobe,
complaining that my constant staring
makes it feel naked,
And I find myself out in the street
interrogating raindrops
as to your whereabouts.
This one particular raindrop
keeps being very evasive
answering in metaphors,
(I may have to get rough).
Happiness stumbles along
smelling of Mad Dog
and mumbo sauce,
wearing cheap sneakers
with holes the size
of a headache
and a shirt that reads

like a menu of stains.
I've begun bottling my tears,
to serve as holy water,
and all the vowels
of my vocabulary
are now lookouts
on my windowsill,
waiting to trumpet
your return.

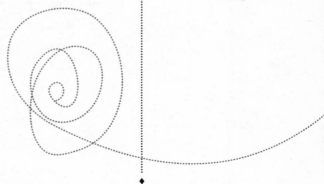

By the Time I Get to Phoenix

The mythical phoenix, when it gets old, burns up. And Shakespeare ain't feeling any younger either. Lucky for him, like the phoenix, new life — in the form of undying art — is ready to spring from the ashes.

Choirs = Benches, like the ruined monastery quires that dot the English countryside, which were full of singers in Catholic England only a few decades before Shakespeare was born.

"THAT TIME OF YEAR THOU MAYST IN ME BEHOLD"

William Shakespeare

That time of year thou mayst in me behold
When yellow leaves, or none, or few, do hang
Upon those boughs which shake against the cold,
Bare ruin'd choirs, where late the sweet birds sang.
In me thou seest the twilight of such day
As after sunset fadeth in the west,
Which by and by black night doth take away,
Death's second self, that seals up all in rest.
In me thou seest the glowing of such fire
That on the ashes of his youth doth lie,
As the death-bed whereon it must expire,
Consum'd with that which it was nourish'd by.
    This thou perceiv'st, which makes thy love more
      strong,
    To love that well, which thou must leave ere long.

GOOD NIGHT

W. S. Merwin

Sleep softly my old love
my beauty in the dark
night is a dream we have
as you know as you know

night is a dream you know
an old love in the dark
around you as you go
without end as you know

in the night where you go
sleep softly my old love
without end in the dark
in the love that you know

Going Gentle

The Welsh poet Dylan Thomas famously pleaded with his dying father not to "go gentle into that good night." In this poem, which evokes Thomas's poem through its title and its repetitive, incantatory structure (something common to many Welsh verse forms), W. S. Merwin seems not to find the prospect of nightfall quite so worrisome as he and his old love approach it.

9 | A FAILURE TO COMMUNICATE

*"Then you should say what you mean," the March
Hare went on.*

*"I do," Alice hastily replied; "at least——at least I
mean what I say—— That's the same thing, you know."*

*"Not the same thing a bit!" said the Hatter.
"Why, you might just as well say that 'I see what I eat' is
the same thing as 'I eat what I see'!"*

—— Lewis Carroll, *Alice's Adventures in Wonderland*

Never Pain to Tell Thy Love

William Blake

Never pain to tell thy Love
Love that never told can be
For the gentle wind does move
Silently invisibly.

I told my love I told my love,
I told her all my heart
Trembling cold in ghastly fears
Ah! she doth depart

Soon as she was gone from me
A traveller came by
Silently invisibly:
O was no deny

Good communication, counselors will tell you, is the key to a lasting relationship. Poets, being poets, would prefer to let their poems do the talking for them — which should be the same thing but somehow isn't. Any wonder that there are so many poems about broken hearts?

Too Much Information

Writing teachers try to drill into their students the principle that it's better to show than to tell. Readers prefer dealing with the concrete and specific than with abstract notions (such as "love"). Here William Blake learns the consequences of too much tell and not enough show.

Pain = Attempt.

You Say I Love Not

Robert Herrick

Y ou say I love not, 'cause I do not play
Still with your curls and kiss the time away.
You blame me, too, because I can't devise
Some sport to please those babies in your eyes:
By Love's religion, I must here confess it,
The most I love when I the least express it.
Small griefs find tongues; full casks are ever found
To give, if any, yet but little sound.
Deep waters noiseless are; and this we know,
That chiding streams betray small depths below.
So when Love speechless is she doth express
A depth in love, and that depth bottomless.
Now since my love is tongueless, know me such,
Who speak but little 'cause I love so much.

Quiet Waters Run Deep

Hollywood suggests that most women prefer the strong, silent types. Such, at least, would be Robert Herrick's hope, as he argues in this sonnet. Somehow his words ring hollow.

Full casks = An empty barrel makes a loud noise when "thunked"; not so one that's full.

The Love Song of J. Alfred Prufrock

T. S. Eliot

EMPTY WORDS

Emerson called poetry "a meter-making argument." Sadly, the evidence of the ages suggests that it's nearly impossible to argue someone into love. Rhetoric is what poets have to work with, though. T. S. Eliot and W. B. Yeats are two of modern literature's most eloquent arguers. See what good it does them in the next two poems.

S'io credessi = *In this prefatory excerpt from Dante's* Inferno, *a spirit in hell agrees to speak candidly, thinking that he's talking to one of the damned. Prufrock's in much the same situation, his doubt and self-loathing coming through.*

S'io credessi che mia risposta fosse
a persona che mai tornasse al mondo,
questa fiamma staria senza più scosse.
Ma per ciò che giammai di questo fondo
non torno vivo alcun, s'i'odo il vero,
senza tema d'infamia ti rispondo.

Let us go then, you and I,
When the evening is spread out against the sky
Like a patient etherised upon a table;
Let us go, through certain half-deserted streets,
The muttering retreats
Of restless nights in one-night cheap hotels
And sawdust restaurants with oyster-shells:
Streets that follow like a tedious argument
Of insidious intent
To lead you to an overwhelming question . . .
Oh, do not ask, "What is it?"
Let us go and make our visit.

In the room the women come and go
Talking of Michelangelo.

The yellow fog that rubs its back upon the window-panes,
The yellow smoke that rubs its muzzle on the window-panes,
Licked its tongue into the corners of the evening,
Lingered upon the pools that stand in drains,
Let fall upon its back the soot that falls from chimneys,
Slipped by the terrace, made a sudden leap,
And seeing that it was a soft October night,
Curled once about the house, and fell asleep.

And indeed there will be time
For the yellow smoke that slides along the street
Rubbing its back upon the window-panes;
There will be time, there will be time
To prepare a face to meet the faces that you meet;
There will be time to murder and create,
And time for all the works and days of hands
That lift and drop a question on your plate;
Time for you and time for me,
And time yet for a hundred indecisions,
And for a hundred visions and revisions,
Before the taking of a toast and tea.

Let us go = *It may help to imagine Prufrock walking through town on the way to a tea party, probably talking to himself, or an imaginary companion from among the damned.*

Like a patient = *He begins with a showy and inappropriate simile, and follows up with several more gloomy, hopeless figures of speech.*

Question = *Just as he's building up to a rhetorical point, he is interrupted by an imagined "stupid" question.*

In the room = *This image distracts him for a moment.*

The yellow fog = *Another fumbling figure of speech — metaphor this time. Eliot, a cat lover, was the author of* Old Possum's Book of Practical Cats, *from which was derived Andrew Lloyd Webber's musical* Cats.

---

*It's often said that Eliot's
famous "love song" isn't a
love song at all. But let's give
Old Possum the benefit of the
doubt here: it's a love song,
just Prufrock's inept one.
Prufrock, the character who's
speaking (or singing) it, is a
showy rhetorician but a lousy
troubadour. Try reading the
poem as if you're someone try-
ing every rhetorical trick in
your arsenal to connect — to
no avail.*

*There will be time =
Prufrock frets about the party
and gets all tangled up in
his rhetoric, anticipating
"stupid" questions like the one
just asked.*

*Morning coat = He considers
being a no-show at
the party, then turns to
another form of communica-
tion — fashion and clothing.
But, again, he fears he will
be misunderstood.*

In the room the women come and go
Talking of Michelangelo.

And indeed there will be time
To wonder, "Do I dare?" and, "Do I dare?"
Time to turn back and descend the stair,
With a bald spot in the middle of my hair —
(They will say: "How his hair is growing thin!")
My morning coat, my collar mounting firmly to the chin,
My necktie rich and modest, but asserted by a simple
   pin —
(They will say: "But how his arms and legs are thin!")
Do I dare
Disturb the universe?
In a minute there is time
For decisions and revisions which a minute will reverse.

For I have known them all already, known them all —
Have known the evenings, mornings, afternoons,
I have measured out my life with coffee spoons;
I know the voices dying with a dying fall
Beneath the music from a farther room.
    So how should I presume?

And I have known the eyes already, known them all—
The eyes that fix you in a formulated phrase,
And when I am formulated, sprawling on a pin,
When I am pinned and wriggling on the wall,
Then how should I begin
To spit out all the butt-ends of my days and ways?
    And how should I presume?

And I have known the arms already, known them all—
Arms that are braceleted and white and bare
(But in the lamplight, downed with light brown hair!)
It is perfume from a dress
That makes me so digress?
Arms that lie along a table, or wrap about a shawl.
    And should I then presume?
    And how should I begin?

. . . .

Shall I say, I have gone at dusk through narrow streets
And watched the smoke that rises from the pipes
Of lonely men in shirt-sleeves, leaning out of
    windows? . . .

Universe = *Here, a moment of bombast, followed immediately by two lines muttered to himself.*

Known them all = *Prufrock's voice now goes Shakespearian and prophetic, like John the Baptist's, including a reference (*dying fall*) to Shakespeare's plays, followed immediately by another moment of doubt.*

The eyes = *Again he speaks with the voice of prophecy, another failed rhetorical mode.*

The arms = *Sex can be a kind of communication, and it is an argument that overwhelms Prufrock.*

Shall I say = *He tries to sum up his earlier rhetorical points, and realizes how hollow it sounds.*

I should have been a pair of ragged claws
Scuttling across the floors of silent seas.

.   .   .   .

And the afternoon, the evening, sleeps so peacefully!
Smoothed by long fingers,
Asleep . . . tired . . . or it malingers,
Stretched on the floor, here beside you and me.
Should I, after tea and cakes and ices,
Have the strength to force the moment to its crisis?
But though I have wept and fasted, wept and prayed,
Though I have seen my head (grown slightly bald) brought
    in upon a platter,
I am no prophet — and here's no great matter;
I have seen the moment of my greatness flicker,
And I have seen the eternal Footman hold my coat, and
    snicker,
And in short, I was afraid.

And would it have been worth it, after all,
After the cups, the marmalade, the tea,
Among the porcelain, among some talk of you and me,
Would it have been worth while,

Ragged claws = *He mutters this, beginning to suspect that language is useless.*

Smoothed = *Once more, the image of the cat.*

Platter = *John the Baptist's head is said to have been cut off and brought on a platter to the lovely Salome, at her request.*

To have bitten off the matter with a smile,
To have squeezed the universe into a ball
To roll it towards some overwhelming question,
To say: "I am Lazarus, come from the dead,
Come back to tell you all, I shall tell you all"—
If one, settling a pillow by her head,
    Should say: "That is not what I meant at all.
    That is not it, at all."

And would it have been worth it, after all,
Would it have been worth while,
After the sunsets and the dooryards and the sprinkled
    streets,
After the novels, after the teacups, after the skirts that trail
    along the floor—
And this, and so much more?—
It is impossible to say just what I mean!
But as if a magic lantern threw the nerves in patterns
    on a screen:
Would it have been worth while
If one, settling a pillow or throwing off a shawl,
And turning toward the window, should say:
    "That is not it at all,
    That is not what I meant, at all."

*Lazarus = Again the pro-
phetic voice is futile; he would
not be understood.*

*Magic lantern = He imagines
a sort of X-ray machine that
can shine through him and
project his innermost thoughts
and feelings for all to see —
but even then he fears he
would be misunderstood.*

. . . .

No! I am not Prince Hamlet, nor was meant to be;
Am an attendant lord, one that will do
To swell a progress, start a scene or two,
Advise the prince; no doubt, an easy tool,
Deferential, glad to be of use,
Politic, cautious, and meticulous;
Full of high sentence, but a bit obtuse;
At times, indeed, almost ridiculous —
Almost, at times, the Fool.

I grow old . . . I grow old . . .
I shall wear the bottoms of my trousers rolled.

Shall I part my hair behind? Do I dare to eat a peach?
I shall wear white flannel trousers, and walk upon the
    beach.
I have heard the mermaids singing, each to each.

I grow old = *This is muttered
again.*

Mermaids = *In mythology,
the singing of mermaids lured
men to their deaths.*

I do not think that they will sing to me.

I have seen them riding seaward on the waves
Combing the white hair of the waves blown back
When the wind blows the water white and black.

We have lingered in the chambers of the sea
By sea-girls wreathed with seaweed red and brown
Till human voices wake us, and we drown.

Human voices = *On this
dispairing note, as Prufrock
utterly gives up on the idea
of communicating with real
women, the poem ends.*

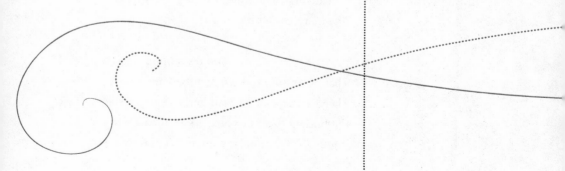

ADAM'S CURSE

W. B. Yeats

An Artsy Crowd

As noted on page 104, Yeats long sought the hand of Maud Gonne, whom he addresses in this poem. Exchanging polite, meaningless words about art and beauty with Gonne and a friend, he suddenly realizes how all that hard work of making beautiful things out of his failed pursuit may have been for nothing. Has he wasted years of his life?

Idler = Poets are often considered lazy bums who can't hold a "real" job.

We sat together at one summer's end,
That beautiful mild woman, your close friend,
And you and I, and talked of poetry.
I said, "A line will take us hours maybe;
Yet if it does not seem a moment's thought,
Our stitching and unstitching has been naught.
Better go down upon your marrow-bones
And scrub a kitchen pavement, or break stones
Like an old pauper, in all kinds of weather;
For to articulate sweet sounds together
Is to work harder than all these, and yet
Be thought an idler by the noisy set
Of bankers, schoolmasters, and clergymen
The martyrs call the world."

                              And thereupon
That beautiful mild woman for whose sake
There's many a one shall find out all heartache
On finding that her voice is sweet and low
Replied, "To be born woman is to know —

Although they do not talk of it at school—
That we must labour to be beautiful."

I said, "It's certain there is no fine thing
Since Adam's fall but needs much labouring.
There have been lovers who thought love should be
So much compounded of high courtesy
That they would sigh and quote with learned looks
Precedents out of beautiful old books;
Yet now it seems an idle trade enough."

We sat grown quiet at the name of love;
We saw the last embers of daylight die,
And in the trembling blue-green of the sky
A moon, worn as if it had been a shell
Washed by time's waters as they rose and fell
About the stars and broke in days and years.

I had a thought for no one's but your ears:
That you were beautiful, and that I strove
To love you in the old high way of love;
That it had all seemed happy, and yet we'd grown
As weary-hearted as that hollow moon.

FIRE AND ICE

Robert Frost

THE COLD SHOULDER

*Indifference can produce
excruciating hurt. These two
poems manage to convey its
effect in all its iciness.*

Desire and Hate

*Robert Frost was a prickly
character, and his plain-
spoken poems sometimes
hide deep alienation,
as in this short reflection,
which is not really about
the end of the world.*

Some say the world will end in fire,
Some say in ice.
From what I've tasted of desire
I hold with those who favor fire.
But if it had to perish twice,
I think I know enough of hate
To say that for destruction ice
Is also great
And would suffice.

"After great pain, a formal feeling comes"

Emily Dickinson

A fter great pain, a formal feeling comes—
The Nerves sit ceremonious, like Tombs—
The stiff Heart questions was it He, that bore,
And Yesterday, or Centuries before?

The Feet, mechanical, go round—
Of Ground, or Air, or Ought—
A Wooden way
Regardless grown,
A Quartz contentment, like a stone—

This is the Hour of Lead—
Remembered, if outlived,
As Freezing persons, recollect the Snow—
First—Chill—then Stupor—then the letting go—

Letting Go

The numbness of failed connection — whether spiritual or romantic is not clear here — suffusing these lines seems worlds away from the ecstatic desire to connect on page 24. Which is why, perhaps, both poems ring so true.

Ought = *Nothing.*

"SINCE THE MAJORITY OF ME"

Philip Larkin

SOUR TASTES

Miscommunication makes for recrimination. As a rule, poets do recrimination quite well and have a lot of practice at it. Here are bitter love poems from two of the best.

A Parliament of Fools

Parliament comes from a root that means to talk, but when the talking ends, what's left unsaid doesn't go away. Perhaps that's why Philip Larkin finds a parliament a useful image for broken love, with a few back-benchers always ready to defy the party line.

Since the majority of me
Rejects the majority of you,
Debating ends forthwith, and we
Divide. And sure of what to do

We disinfect new blocks of days
For our majorities to rent
With unshared friends and unwalked ways.
But silence too is eloquent:

A silence of minorities
That, unopposed at last, return
Each night with cancelled promises
They want renewed. They never learn.

THE RIVAL

Sylvia Plath

If the moon smiled, she would resemble you.
You leave the same impression
Of something beautiful, but annihilating.
Both of you are great light borrowers.
Her O-mouth grieves at the world; yours is unaffected,

And your first gift is making stone out of everything.
I wake to a mausoleum; you are here,
Ticking your fingers on the marble table, looking for
    cigarettes,
Spiteful as a woman, but not so nervous,
And dying to say something unanswerable.

The moon, too, abases her subjects,
But in the daytime she is ridiculous.
Your dissatisfactions, on the other hand,

**With Friends
Like You . . .**

*Even bright moonlight sucks
the colors out of a landscape,
which seems to be Plath's
complaint about the re-
flected brilliance of her lover
here — presumably her hus-
band, the poet Ted Hughes.
The lesson for poets is simple:
don't marry another poet.*

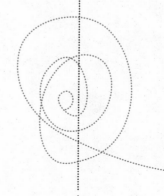

Arrive through the mailslot with loving regularity,
White and blank, expansive as carbon monoxide.

No day is safe from news of you,
Walking about in Africa maybe, but thinking of me.

Carbon monoxide = *An
odorless poison gas.*

THE LOST MISTRESS

Robert Browning

All's over, then: does truth sound bitter
    As one at first believes?
Hark, 'tis the sparrows' good-night twitter
    About your cottage eaves!

And the leaf-buds on the vine are woolly,
    I noticed that, to-day;
One day more bursts them open fully
    — You know the red turns grey.

To-morrow we meet the same then, dearest?
    May I take your hand in mine?
Mere friends are we, — well, friends the merest
    Keep much that I resign:

For each glance of that eye so bright and black,
    Though I keep with heart's endeavour, —
Your voice, when you wish the snowdrops back,
    Though it stay in my soul for ever! —

FRIENDS AND LOVERS

Can ex-lovers stay friends? Can friendship continue between lovers? Poets keep trying to answer questions like these, but the answers remain ambiguous. In these poems, Robert Browning tries ignoring his feelings and putting on a civil public face, while John Updike entertains a moment of alienation in the privacy of a shared bed.

Yet I will but say what mere friends say,
        Or only a thought stronger;
I will hold your hand but as long as all may,
        Or so very little longer!

Second Thoughts

Victorian gentlemen were so polite! Here, the need to appear civilized forces the poet to bite back deeper feelings.

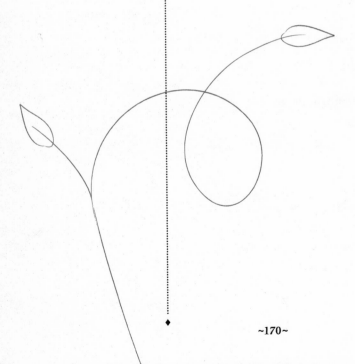

Sleeping with You

John Updike

One creature, not the mollusk
clamped around an orgasm, but
more loosely biune, we are linked
by tugs of the blanket and dreams whose disquiet
unsettles night's oily depths, creating
those eddies of semi-wakefulness wherein
we acknowledge the other is there
as an arm is there, or an ancestor,
or any fact admitted yet not known.

What body is warm beside mine,
what corpse has been slain
on this soft battlefield where we wounded
lift our heads to cry for water
and ask what forces prevailed?
It is you, not dead, but entrusted
at my side to the flight the chemical mind
must take or be crazed, leaving the body
behind like matériel in a trench.

An Imperfect Fit

Waking up in the middle of the night, while his lover sleeps and dreams, Updike finds both alienation and union in the trust of two people sharing the same bed.

Mollusk = *A hinged shellfish, such as a clam.*

Biune = *Consisting of two combined in one.*

Corpse = *The imagery is that of World War I trench warfare.*

Chemical mind = *Going without dreaming sleep for extended periods produces imbalances in brain chemistry that lead to psychosis.*

Matériel = *War supplies.*

The moon throws back sunlight into the woods,
but whiter, cleansed by its bounce
amid the cold stars, and the owls
fly their unthinkable paths to pluck
the velvet mole from her tunnel of leaves.
Dreaming rotates us, but fear
leads us to cling each to each as a spar
is clung to by the shipwrecked
till dawn brings sky-fire and rescue.

Your breathing, relaxed to its center,
scrapes like a stone on rough fiber,
over and over. Your skin, steeped
in its forgetting, sweats,
and flurries of footwork bring you near
the surface; but then your rapt lungs slip
with a sigh back into the healing,
that unpoliced swirling of spirit
whose sharing is a synonym for love.

10 | SECOND TIME AROUND

Go and leave me if you wish to.
Never let it cross your mind.
If in your heart you love another
leave me little darling, I don't mind.

— "Columbus Stockade Blues," Traditional

"SINCE THERE'S NO HELP, COME, LET US KISS AND PART"

Michael Drayton

ENDINGS AND
BEGINNINGS

---

*How many lovers have broken
up only to get back together?
That's the direction in which
Michael Drayton's heading.
But William Shakespeare sug-
gests that you might as well
keep walking, make a clean
break and get on to the
next thing.*

Doctor, Doctor!

---

*"Physician, heal thyself!" the
Gospel advises. "The heck with
that," the Elizabethan poet
Drayton replies in this sonnet
from* Idea. *"Heal me."*

Since there's no help, come, let us kiss and part.
Nay, I have done, you get no more of me,
And I am glad, yea glad with all my heart
That thus so cleanly I myself can free;
Shake hands forever, cancel all our vows,
And when we meet at any time again
Be it not seen in either of our brows
That we one jot of former love retain.
Now at the last gasp of Love's latest breath,
When, his pulse failing, Passion speechless lies,
When Faith is kneeling by his bed of death
And Innocence is closing up his eyes,
    Now if thou would'st, when all have given him over,
    From death to life thou might'st him yet recover.

"Sigh No More, Ladies" (*from* Much Ado About Nothing)

William Shakespeare

Sigh no more, ladies, sigh no more,
   Men were deceivers ever,
One foot in sea, and one on shore,
   To one thing constant never.
Then sigh not so, but let them go,
   And be you blithe and bonny,
Converting all your sounds of woe
   Into hey nonny nonny.

Sing no more ditties, sing no moe,
   Of dumps so dull and heavy;
The fraud of men was ever so,
   Since summer first was leavy.
Then sigh not so, but let them go,
   And be you blithe and bonny,
Converting all your sounds of woe
   Into hey nonny nonny.

Nothing New under the Sun

Shakespeare's take draws more on the wisdom of the Old Testament book of Ecclesiastes. As much as we try to understand and control the world, finally it's futile. So, with faith and hope, we accept what's past and cheerfully move on to what's next.

Hey nonny nonny = A medieval nonsense phrase, which Shakespeare uses to suggest words like nonce and anon that convey the nowness of love.

Moe = More.

Dumps = Depression.

Leavy = Leafy.

Sources of the Delaware

Dean Young

I love you he said but saying it took twenty years
so it was like listening to mountains grow.
I love you she says fifty times into a balloon
then releases the balloon into a room
whose volume she calculated to fit
the breath it would take to read
the complete works of Charlotte Bronte aloud.
Someone else pours green dust into the entryway
and puts rice paper on the floor. The door
is painted black. On the clothesline
shirttails snap above the berserk daffodils.
Hoagland says you've got to plunge the sword
into the charging bull. You've got
to sew yourself into a suit of light.
For the vacuum tube, it's easy,
just heat the metal to incandescence
and all that dark energy becomes radiance.
A kind of hatching, syntactic and full of buzz.
No contraindications, no laws forbidding

buying gin on Sundays. No if you're pregnant,
if you're operating heavy machinery because
who isn't towing the scuttled tonnage
of some self? Sometimes just rubbing
her feet is enough. Just putting out
a new cake of soap. Sure, the contents
are under pressure and everyone knows
that last step was never intended to bear
any weight but isn't that why we're standing there?
Ripples in her hair, I love you she hollers
over the propellers. Yellow scarf in mist.
When I planted all those daffodils,
I didn't know I was planting them
in my own chest. Play irretrievably
with the lid closed, Satie wrote on the score.
But Hoagland says he's sick of opening
the door each morning not on diamonds
but piles of coal, and he's sick of being
responsible for the eons of pressure needed
and the sea is sick of being responsible
for the rain, and the river is sick of the sea.
So the people who need the river
to float waste to New Jersey

Like a River

*Dean Young wrote that a
sense of an "unavoidable and
unopposable forward flood" of
images led him to make this
a love poem. Notice how they
swirl and eddy with the cur-
rent, somehow united in the
direction they're going.*

Satie = *French composer Erik
Satie (1866 – 1925).*

Coal = *Diamonds and coal
are both produced by pressure
on carbon deposits.*

throw in antidepressants. So the river
is still sick but nervous now too,
its legs keep thrashing out involuntarily,
flooding going concerns, keeping the president
awake. So the people throw in beta-blockers
to make it sleep which it does, sort of,
dreaming it's a snake again but this time
with fifty heads belching ammonia
which is nothing like the dreams it once had
of children splashing in the blue of its eyes.
So the president gets on the airways
with positive vectors and vows
to give every child a computer
but all this time, behind the podium,
his penis is shouting, Put me in, Coach,
I can be the river! So I love you say
the flashbulbs but then the captions
say something else. I love you says
the hammer to the nail. I love Tamescha
someone sprays across the For Sale sign.
So I tell Hoagland it's a fucked-up ruined
world in such palatial detail, he's stuck
for hours on the phone. Look at those crows,

Beta-blockers = *Drugs that moderate the heartbeat and lower blood pressure.*

they think they're in on the joke and
they don't love a thing. They think
they have to be that black to keep
all their radiance inside. I love you
the man says as his mother dies
so now nothing ties him to the earth,
not fistfuls of dirt, not the silly songs
he remembers singing as a child.
I love you I say meaning lend me twenty bucks.

December at Yase

Gary Snyder

You said, that October,
In the tall dry grass by the orchard
When you chose to be free,
"Again someday, maybe ten years."

After college I saw you
One time. You were strange,
And I was obsessed with a plan.

Now ten years and more have
Gone by: I've always known
        where you were —
I might have gone to you
Hoping to win your love back.
You still are single.

I didn't.
I thought I must make it alone. I
Have done that.

Only in dream, like this dawn,
Does the grave, awed intensity
Of our young love
Return to my mind, to my flesh.

We had what the others
All crave and seek for;
We left it behind at nineteen.

I feel ancient, as though I had
Lived many lives.

And may never now know
If I am a fool
Or have done what my
    karma demands.

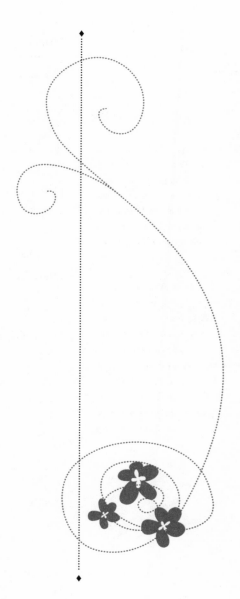

FREEDOM

Jan Struther

Now, heaven be thanked, I am out of love again!
　　I have been long a slave, and now am free;
I have been tortured, and am eased of pain;
　　I have been blind, and now my eyes can see;
I have been lost, and now the way lies plain;
　　I have been caged, and now I hold the key;
I have been mad, and now at last am sane;
　　I am wholly I, that was but a half of me.
　　So, a free man, my dull proud path I plod,
　　Who, tortured, blind, mad, caged, was once a God.

Good Morning, Love!

Paul Blackburn

To-do List

---

*Here's a glimpse into a day
in the life of Paul Blackburn,
a poet and translator who
was a follower of Ezra Pound.
He wrote this in 1958, at a
time when he had recently
separated from his first wife.
Blackburn went on to marry
twice more.*

Rise at 7:15
study the
artifacts
    (2 books
    1 photo
    1 gouache sketch
    2 unclean socks
perform the neces-
sary ablutions
    hands
    face, feet
    crotch
even answer the door
with good grace, even
if it's the light-and-gas man
announcing himself as "EDISON!
Readjer meter, mister?"

For Chrissake yes
        read my meter
        Nothing can alter the euphoria
The blister is still on one finger
        There just are
some mornings worth getting up
& making a cup
of coffee,
            that's all

I So Liked Spring

Charlotte Mew

I so liked Spring last year
    Because you were here;—
        The thrushes too—
Because it was these you so liked to hear—
        I so liked you.

    This year's a different thing,—
        I'll not think of you.
But I'll like Spring because it is simply Spring
        As the thrushes do.

LOOKING FORWARD, LOOKING BACK

The next two poems are about getting over lost love. One poet finds it easy. The other doesn't.

Kindred Souls

During the Edwardian era, when she published, Thomas Hardy called Charlotte Mew "far and away the best living woman poet." She's not much remembered today, but she shared with Hardy a poetic vision in which nature, independent of any divine purpose, becomes a common reference by which we define ourselves.

I LOOK INTO MY GLASS

Thomas Hardy

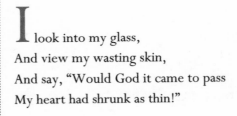

I look into my glass,
And view my wasting skin,
And say, "Would God it came to pass
My heart had shrunk as thin!"

For then, I, undistrest
By hearts grown cold to me,
Could lonely wait my endless rest
With equanimity.

But Time, to make me grieve,
Part steals, lets part abide;
And shakes this fragile frame at eve
With throbbings of noontide.

Hearts Grown Full

Hardy wrote several memorable poems about thrushes. This is not one of those, but it's memorable in its own right. It may seem like an older man's poem (Hardy wrote powerful poetry up until the very end, dying in 1928 at age 88), but in fact it's among his earliest. The heart, it seems, doesn't age as quickly as the skin.

AN ANSWER TO A LOVE LETTER IN VERSE

Lady Mary Wortley Montagu

Is it to me, this sad-lamenting strain?
Are heaven's choicest gifts bestow'd in vain?
A plenteous fortune, and a beauteous bride,
Your love rewarded, and content your pride!
Yet leaving her — 'tis me that you pursue,
Without one single charm, but being new.

    How vile is man! How I detest the ways
Of artful falsehood, and designing praise!
Tasteless, an easy happiness you slight,
Ruin your joy, and mischief your delight.
Why should poor pug (the mimic of your kind)
Wear a rough chain, and be to box confin'd?
Some cup perhaps he breaks, or tears a fan,
While moves unpunish'd the destroyer, man.
Not bound by vows, and unrestrain'd by shame,
In sport you break the heart, and rend the fame.
Not that your art can be successful here,
Th' already plunder'd need no robber fear,
Nor sighs, nor charms, nor flattery can move,

LESSONS LEARNED, AND NOT

Experience is a powerful teacher, but even with its lessons firmly in mind, people have the bad habit of making the same mistakes over and over again. Neither of these two voices of experience seems completely ready to declare itself immune to the attractions of love.

Pug = *A monkey.*

Robber = *An important image for this poem. During this period, robbers and highwaymen (the "gangstas" of their day) were a hazard for travelers — especially a woman on her own.*

It's an Old Rap, Dawg

Have some fun and try reading this eighteenth-century poem as if it were a hip-hop lyric. In many ways, the stylized "heroic couplets" of the era resemble today's rap songs. Montagu was best known as a letter-writer, but she also wrote poetry with a sharp, satirical edge to it.

Brisk wits = *Jovial highway robbers.*

Justice = *After they've been arrested.*

Too well secur'd against a second love.
Once, and but once, that devil charm'd my mind,
To reason deaf, to observation blind,
I idly hop'd (what cannot love persuade?)
My fondness equall'd, and my truth repaid,
Slow to distrust, and willing to believe,
Long hush'd my doubts, and would my self deceive;
But oh too soon — this tale would ever last,
Sleep, sleep my wrongs, and let me think 'em past.

 For you who mourn with counterfeited grief
And ask so boldly like a begging thief;
May soon some other nymph inflict the pain
You know so well, with cruel art to feign,
Tho' long you've sported with Don Cupid's dart,
You may see eyes, and you may feel a heart.

 So the brisk wits who stop the evening coach
Laugh at the fear that follows their approach,
With idle mirth, and haughty scorn despise
The passenger's pale cheek, and staring eyes;
But seiz'd by Justice, find a fright no jest
And all the terror doubled in their breast.

SYMPTOM RECITAL

Dorothy Parker

I do not like my state of mind;
I'm bitter, querulous, unkind.
I hate my legs, I hate my hands,
I do not yearn for lovelier lands.
I dread the dawn's recurrent light;
I hate to go to bed at night.
I snoot at simple, earnest folk.
I cannot take the gentlest joke.
I find no peace in paint or type.
My world is but a lot of tripe.
I'm disillusioned, empty-breasted.
For what I think, I'd be arrested.
I am not sick, I am not well.
My quondam dreams are shot to hell.
My soul is crushed, my spirit sore;
I do not like me any more.
I cavil, quarrel, grumble, grouse.
I ponder on the narrow house.
I shudder at the thought of men. . . .
I'm due to fall in love again.

Mirror, Mirror

Ah, love! It has been quite a journey. And, as we end our trip through this amorous landscape of love poetry, perhaps we should let Dorothy Parker, denizen of the urban jungle, have the last word, as she diagnoses herself.

Quondam = *Former.*

INDEX OF TITLES

INDEX OF FIRST LINES

Index of Authors